Reasons for Hope

Reasons for Hope

José Luis Martín Descalzo

Translated by David Gray

Fortress Press
Minneapolis

Ediciones Sígueme
Salamanca

REASONS FOR HOPE

Cover photo © Steve Edson Photography, Inc./Getty Images
Cover and book design by Douglas Schmitz

Library of Congress Cataloging-in-Publication Data
Martín Descalzo, José Luis, 1930–1991
  [Razones para la esperanza. English]
  Reasons for hope / José Luis Martín Descalzo; translated by David Gray.
    p. cm.
  ISBN 978-0-8006-6223-3 (alk. paper)
  1. Christian life—Catholic authors. I. Title.
  BX2350.3.M2713 2007
  248.4'82—dc22
                                              2007006518

The paper used in this publication meets the minimum requirements of
American National Standard for Information Sciences—Permanence of
Paper for Printed Library Materials, ANSI Z329.48-1984.

Manufactured in the U.S.A.

11   10   09   08   07   1   2   3   4   5   6   7   8   9   10

CONTENTS

The story of Anne   1

Dear burglar   5

A poor man in the garden   9

Dustcovers   13

Grass grows at night   17

How many battles have you lost, my boy?   21

A dollar for the fruit   25

Don't kill anybody, Son   29

The devil's daughter   33

The six qualities of the honorable man   37

You can't pull strings in heaven   41

"Miss Swimsuit" cannot swim   45

Her eyes were green   49

Replacing my diary   53

Christmas proclamation in a time of fear   57

An insult to heaven   61

The gypsy's miracle   65

The theory of the springboard   69

The terrorist did not sleep last night   73

Queen does not laugh   77

Contents

All parents are foster parents   81

The injured leg   85

The right to make mistakes   89

The war of the smart folk   93

The new slavery   97

"Put your sword away"   101

Ill from loneliness   105

Burning Judas   109

The year that Christ died in the flames   113

A field sown with future   117

The bad guy in the film   121

The sweet kingdom   125

The virtues of *and*   129

Encouraging those who fail   133

Traveling like suitcases   137

Our daily peace   141

In praise of courage   145

"Look after your wings, lad"   149

The heretic and the inquisitor   153

My ten commandments   157

José Luis Martín Descalzo — A Life Sketch   *161*

Index   *165*

The story of Anne

Anne is an elderly widow, a very elderly widow in fact, a most proper widow who lives in a city whose name I prefer not to recall. And what I am about to tell you is an absolutely true story, for all that it might seem to be a fable.

Anne was unfortunate enough to become a widow four days after her wedding, for her husband ("Frank," she calls him) died a lieutenant or a captain, she cannot remember which, in a far-off war in either Africa or Asia—she is not sure. What she does know is that Frank left her with next to nothing: a handsome old photograph, going yellow now; some old silk sheets, which were only used for four nights; and a pension of a hundred dollars and a few cents.

And on this princely sum Anne survives, a gazelle from prehistoric times in a world populated by monsters. But Anne manages to make her hundred dollars last through the month, even taking into account the fact that of course the first thing she does when she gets her pension on the thirtieth of each month is to spend a dollar on a candle that she lights in memory and in honor of Frank.

Some months ago she was paid her pension in a single hundred-dollar bill. Anne was delighted with the hundred-dollar bill, for it was the first time she had had one, and to her it was like winning the lottery. But at the same time she was beset by the most acute attack of nerves at the thought that she might lose it. She would not be happy until she had changed it the next morning in the shop.

And the attack of nerves returned the following day, when she went to pay for the vegetables she had bought after mass. For she discovered that in spite of all her precautions, or perhaps because of them, the money had disappeared. She searched through her bag and turned it inside out. Nothing. She went back no fewer than five times over the route she had taken from her house to the church and from the church to the market. Nothing. She looked under all the pews in the church and pushed aside all the furniture in her house to see underneath. Still nothing.

And now she was invaded by the most terrible anxiety. How was she going to get through those thirty awful, endless days till the end of the month when she did not have a cent in the bank and all the people whom she had known in this world had already passed on to the next? She went through all her things again and confirmed once more that there was nothing of value left to sell . . . except of course the ancient silk sheets, a silver coffee service that had been a wedding present from her brothers and sisters, and an old medallion that had belonged to her mother. To sell any of those things would be like selling herself!

She made do that day with the leftovers from her old fridge and hardly slept at all that night. At one point, in a brief moment between one anxious dream and the next, the thought came to her: "That's it, I must have lost it in the elevator, when I was going down to mass!" She got up shivering, put a coat on over her nightdress, and went out onto the stairs. But there was nothing either on the stairs or in the elevator. And she went back to bed like a woman who has just had her death sentence confirmed.

The next morning, on her way to mass (God was all that was left to her now), she put a little sign up in the elevator saying that if anyone had found a hundred-dollar bill, could they please return it to her. But she did it convinced in her heart that it was hopeless.

That was the saddest mass she had ever attended. When the priest began to pray the penitential rite, our most proper widow remembered how, in one of her comings and goings the day before, she had passed the other widow from the fourth floor on the stairs, the one whom all the neighbors called the merry widow, to distinguish her from Anne (and apparently the name was well deserved, from what people said). Anne remembered that the other widow had been carrying a beautiful new leather bag. That was where her money must have gone! It was as clear as the light of day!

But then, as the priest was reading from the Gospel, Anne remembered the two girls who lived on the third floor, the two who came back late every night with their boyfriends on big noisy motorcycles, and how the previous night they had come back even later than usual. She shuddered at the mere thought of what those two hussies might have done with her hundred dollars!

As the priest recited the offertory, she thought of the man who lived on the second floor, the butcher, a sour-faced communist whom she had met on the stairs yesterday and who had given her a nasty gloating look. Good God, what use might that communist have put her money to?

During the blessing it was the turn of Fred, the one whom they reckoned lived with a woman who was not his wife, to become the target of Anne's suspicions. And since the mass went on for another ten minutes, Anne had plenty of time to go through all her neighbors, one by one, and convince herself that every single one of them had almost certainly appropriated the money that was her very lifeblood.

By the time she got back home, Anne was furious at the thought of living in a building that was such a pit of corruption. She went to open the door of her apartment, but as she did so, she slipped and dropped her missal. Twelve little votive cards and a hundred-dollar bill fell out. And quite suddenly it came to her that she was the one to blame, stupid woman that she was, and that all her suffering had been her own fault.

Just as she was getting ready to go to the market, on top of the world now, the doorbell rang. It was the widow from the fourth floor, who, just imagine, had found the money the day before in the elevator. And when she left, excusing herself and saying that somebody else living in the building must have dropped it, the two girls from the third floor came up and said that, amazingly, they had found a hundred dollars on the stairs as well. Next it was the butcher. He had not found the bill, but he wanted her to take five twenty-dollar bills wrapped in a little bundle. Then Fred came up, and a dozen more neighbors, and the funny thing was that they had all found the money on the stairs!

Anne could only cry for joy. For she realized that the world is a beautiful place and that people are good, and that she had only been polluting the world with the meanness of her fear.

Dear burglar

I hope these lines of my notebook fall into your hands one day, my burglar friend. Two weeks ago you broke open my front door, searched through all my drawers, and opened every last one of my cupboards. The least I can do is to thank you, not so much because you did not take anything, but because you did not touch a single one of my papers.

I suppose, my boy—for I am sure that you are not much more than a boy—I suppose that you must have cursed your luck when you discovered (unfortunately for you, happily for me) that in my house there was nothing of any interest to you: only books, music, and the odd piece of art of considerable sentimental value though of no great monetary worth. You were looking for jewelry, gold, or money, I suppose, to sink yourself deeper into the hell of drugs. You could have saved yourself the trouble of smashing the door frame if you had known what kind of person I am. You would have known that I regard gold and jewelry as the two stupidest things in the world. And that as far as money is concerned, I have the devilish ability to spend it faster than I make it. You couldn't find what wasn't there. And yet in spite of it all . . .

In spite of it all, you took from me something much more valuable than diamonds—with the help of my cowardliness, naturally. Let me explain.

I have always maintained that trust is an integral part of human life, that rather than live with an armor-plated soul, it would be better not to live at all. If I cannot trust those around me, if I put up a barrier of barbed wire around my life and around my heart, I am not hurting the people who come close to me. I am hurting myself. An untrusting heart gets old quickly. A heart that is shut up tight is deader than a heart whose owner has already passed away.

That is why I always refused to have my doors reinforced (which is the reason that you had so little trouble in forcing them). And that is also why I have always had the habit of leaving the keys in the locks of drawers and cupboards (which is the reason that you did not have to smash them open).

The three neighbors who share a landing with me in the building where I live had already had the front doors of their houses reinforced. All three of them had often told me to do the same, for every day they read reports in the papers about boys like you. I always laughed. "In my house," I used to tell them, "there is nothing of interest to a burglar." But deep within myself, I was aware that this was not the real reason. Of course I knew that violence is one of the great drivers of the world, but I did not want to face up to the fact, or at least I preferred to imagine that it would never affect me directly. And, of course, I never thought that it could turn me into a practitioner of "defensive violence" or make a closed soul of me.

There was another reason as well. If you knew me, you would be aware of the fact that I have always considered Georges Bernanos as something of a spiritual father.

Now Bernanos (I recommend you to read him, by the way; he is a lot more exciting than drugs) absolutely worshiped the idea of trust between people. So much so, that when someone told him about an area of Brazil where the houses have neither doors nor locks nor keys, he went off to live there, convinced that people who think like that must be truly rounded human beings.

I have always felt attracted to this idea myself. I even preferred to be robbed rather than fortify my soul like a castle high on an impregnable rock.

Well, let me tell you: I have given in. I, a sinner, make my confession to you, my burglar friend. Your greed and my cowardliness have proved stronger than all my good intentions.

That evening, when I found my door wide open, thanks to your work, something rose up deep within me. Not against you (or at least not only against you), but against the world that we are building around us. That is why I would like to find out who you are and what you are like. I would like to discover if you are aware, as I am, of just what we are doing to this planet, of how between all of us we are making it completely uninhabitable. The thought that drugs may already have snuffed out your conscience is more than I can bear.

I slept badly that night. Imaginary noises kept waking me up. I kept seeing monsters coming back—monsters who were probably not like you at all, or were like a kind of magnified version of you, or were like you will end up if you go much further down the path you are on. I was overcome by a secret rage. Not because you had broken into my house (really, thinking about it, I should consider myself lucky; after all, you did not take anything), but because we live in a society that perhaps began by shutting the doors of work in your face and then went on to open wide the gates of vice. And not any old vice, but vice of the most expensive and destructive sort.

I continued to feel strange for the next ten days. My heart would start thumping harshly as I got close to home, imagining that I would again find the door forced and that you would be in there, trembling, with a knife or a gun in your hand.

So much for my sense of trust. I gave in on the sixth day, convinced by the devil knows what, that only an armored door could bring peace back to my traumatized heart.

And there they are: locks, bars, steel plates, hugely complicated keys, a whole defensive arsenal. Just as if I lived in a safe-deposit box and I myself had turned into one of those gold bars I abhor so much.

I feel a lot safer now. But a lot less of a person. A lot less brotherly. I do not mind the money that I have had to spend because of you. What I really mind is the knowledge that I have joined the ranks of those who do not trust, who live with their souls overrun by guard dogs.

The fault is not only yours. It is mine too. And this sensation that we are both to blame is the only human lesson that I have taken from this whole business. That is why I hope that you will read these lines, so that you can feel something of the same. Then both of us would realize how your greed and my fear came together to create this sad state of affairs.

A poor man in the garden

Years ago I had a friend who was a member of a small and fervent Christian community. The members used to meet one day a week to talk about Christ, about their faith, and about how to spread its message. Because they were all people who worked eight hours a day, they used to meet at night, have a light dinner, and then stay on talking, sometimes until two or three o'clock in the morning. My friend used to leave those meetings with his soul on fire, the light of the gospel burning bright in him, ready to give the best of his life to his faith. Until one night . . .

It was winter, a bitingly cold night, and my friend got home at close to three in the morning after his conversation with the other members of the community. And when he got out of his car, he saw that across the street from the entrance to the building where he lived, in the garden opposite, a man was asleep on an iron bench, his crumpled body barely covered by a few newspapers.

Something shifted in my friend's soul: on a night like that, a man lying on a bench with only an old overcoat and a few newspapers for protection could very well freeze to death. How could he abandon him just like that? He heard a voice inside his head shouting that that would be a crime. But then another voice told him that he could not take a complete stranger into his house. What if he was a thief? And what would his wife and his children say if he woke them up at three in the morning to find somewhere for that ragged individual to sleep?

As my friend put his key into the lock, he shouted to himself a thousand times that he was being a coward. But his selfishness was too strong for him. And once he got into his apartment, he deliberately avoided looking out over the balcony so that his conscience would not batter him any harder than it was already doing.

When he got into bed, the blankets seemed both warm and freezing at the same time. He felt as if he were living simultaneously in the burning hell of his selfishness and in the freezing body of the beggar. And it was several hours before he could get to sleep, for he could not get the body of the man curled up on the bench out of his mind.

When he woke up the next morning, he went over to the window in a panic: he was sure that he would see the same body that he had left to its fate lying there on the bench, but perhaps dead now. The bench was empty. He did not know whether to laugh or cry.

His shame burned in him the whole of the following week. He looked at himself in the mirror and was disgusted. He did not dare to go to church or to take communion. He could not wait for the following Friday to come so that he could confess to God and his companions the sin that weighed more and more heavily on his conscience as the days went by.

When the Friday eventually came and he was able to tell the story of his cowardice, almost crying as he did so, he was amazed to see that none of his companions seemed particularly affected by what he had to say. It was not just that they made light of the whole thing, saying that everybody makes a thousand mistakes a day; it was that they even managed to come up with all sorts of theories to excuse how he had behaved. Somebody explained that the most pressing battle was not so much to help individuals as to change society. Somebody else said that charity was only authentic when it brought about justice. A third person commented that alms were as degrading for the person receiving them as for the person who gave them. Somebody added that giving a tramp a place to sleep was not going to solve his problems. And of course there was the typical comment: "People like that are used to sleeping on benches."

My friend left the meeting that night more chilled than ever. And he decided never to return to that community. He did not want to pass judgment on them, much less condemn them. But he realized that something was not right there.

I have told this story, which is completely true, because I think it symbolizes the world in which we live. We know so much about society yet forget about human beings, about individual human beings.

I have often wondered why we have lost so much of our sense of sin. I think the answer is that we have all managed to convince ourselves that evil is something anonymous, that it's society's fault, not ours.

Turn on the television any day, and you will see some expert being interviewed about the problems of crime. Straight off you will hear how society is badly structured. Apparently neither the delinquent nor the people around him are to blame at all. "The structures" are at fault; the day the structures change, we are told, crime will disappear. Nobody seems to even know what the structures are.

As you would expect, I am not about to play down the importance that social circumstances have in human behavior. I am well aware that poverty, lack of education, and appalling living conditions are at least 80 percent responsible for a great deal of crime and morally reprehensible behavior. But I cannot avoid noticing two things: first, that a lot of other people surviving in the same poverty, lack of education, and appalling living conditions bravely struggle to be honest; and second, that other people who have enjoyed wealth, a good education, and an easy life sometimes fall into the very same morally reprehensible behavior. My conclusion is that while the circumstances of life can provide the wood for the fire, it is the individual human conscience that generates the spark that sets the wood alight.

Which is why I am deeply wary of any philosophy that does not address the individual human being. Of course I know that an act of generosity does not solve the underlying problem. That it is more important to teach people to fish than to give them a fish. That the person who finds someone a job is a thousand times more effective than the person who gives a dollar a week. But having said that, the idea that we can change the world without loving individual human beings seems to me a load of rubbish, like talking about bringing justice to earth while a man is dying of cold in a garden.

It used to be that cowardice was called cowardice, and selfishness, selfishness. Nowadays I fear that we are using phrases like *intelligent charity, desire for justice,* and *structural reforms* to describe what are nothing more than selfish dreams about ways to shut off the screams of our consciences.

Dustcovers

Do you remember the Graham Greene play called *The Living Room*, in which all the characters lived in permanent fear at the thought of death, and even worse, in horror at the prospect of living? Father James Browne, the spiritually crippled old man, and his equally aged spinster sisters, Helen and Teresa, have no other passions in their lives apart from their fear of death and their flight from everything that might involve life or love. And the house they live in is the offspring of these twin fears, for as their parents and other brothers and sisters have died off over the years, the survivors have gradually sealed up rooms in the house. The door to a room where someone dies is permanently locked and bolted and the furniture is carefully covered in dustcovers. In this way death has slowly taken the house over, room by room, in a kind of hand-to-hand struggle with the people living there. The surviving inhabitants have been expelled from their apartments and forced to huddle together. At the time of the play, they live in a few entirely inadequate rooms while the rest of the huge dwelling, which at one time had various floors, is nothing more than an enormous furniture storeroom, completely empty and inhabited only by the ghastly ghost of death itself.

Greene described a set in which none of the furniture matched, for it is obvious that each piece has been brought from a different part of the house, and in which the living room gave directly onto a ridiculous lavatory. When I first saw the play, many years ago, that set struck me as the visible symbol of thousands of souls, of all those people with huge areas of their lives that are not lived in, whose hearts are nothing more than storerooms for furniture covered in dustcovers.

For I know many people who have gradually trimmed and whittled away at their hearts as the years have gone by.

There was a time when they aspired to doing something with their lives. But then after failing a few times, they drew back into bitterness, allowing their disappointment to harden into scars and sealing up their store of hope, as if it would never again produce anything but dust. Perhaps at some point they had felt something like love and had given themselves to a man or a woman. But then that love failed, perhaps because they were rejected, or perhaps, even worse, because once they were married they discovered that their love was less exciting than they had dreamed. So then they closed up the room of love that they had briefly opened in their souls. Anything that might bring a fresh ray of hope they covered with dustcovers, and they succumbed to that sad way of thinking that holds that the best way to avoid suffering is not to love, for we always suffer when we lose what we love.

Later they sealed off the room of friendship, then the room that they used to work from, and in this way they committed a form of slow suicide, whittling away chunks of their souls, drawing back into a few rooms where selfishness and fear reigned supreme.

Souls like these make a deep impression on me, in the same way as houses that have been uninhabited for years do: the corners are choked with cobwebs; the dust has worked its way in under the sheets, which lend a ghostly air to the furniture. All that remains is for the wind and the rain to batter the windows to shreds, and the whole place will start to have the smell of the graveyard about it. There are souls like this, far too many of them; when they are opened they give off the moldy smell of cupboards that have not been opened for years.

It is not just that people like this commit suicide; they destroy the hopes of anyone who comes close to them. A terrible thing happens in Greene's play: one day someone new arrives at the house of these three miserable creatures, who think that they love God because they love nobody in the world. It is Rose, the sinful niece, who is living a stormy passion with a married man. She has come to ask for help. But what frightens her old uncle and his two spinster sisters is not so much the sin that their niece has committed, but rather the fact that it is a sin of love, something for which there is no room in that house of death and dead people. So Rose is abandoned by her holier-than-thou relatives, and she ends up killing herself in the only room that the frightened threesome has left, and which they should now really seal up as well, in order to flee from the memory of the death that took place there. Their only living room, the place where up until now they had "lived," though perhaps "fossilized" might be a better word.

It is only when Rose commits suicide that the eyes of those three living dead are opened. They discover that the dead can kill, that those who live without love not only kill themselves, but are also poisonous to others. For it is impossible to live in a house inhabited by the memory of the dead, in which even the inhabitants who are alive and who do walk, move around, eat, and speak have souls that have long since been mummified.

The great lesson I learned from that play was that fear builds nothing. It is better to be wrong than to be mummified. Making mistakes is better than constantly running away from everything that is alive. To live avoiding life does not help us to better avoid feeling pain. The day a soul turns into a house in which all hope has been locked away, in which smiles are blinkered, in which hands are not shaken but used to defend oneself, in which all the promises of youth have become nothing more than a collection of furniture covered in dustcovers, in a house like this there is only one hope: that enough humility remains to ask God to come quickly.

Or perhaps . . . ? Yes, perhaps it would be better to hope that enough lucidity remains for us to realize that just as a green shoot could sprout from the elm tree "wounded by lightning," which Antonio Machado wrote of, in spite of the fact that the tree seemed to be dead, so perhaps "some miracle of spring" could sprout among the dustsheet-covered furniture.

Grass grows at night

I do not know who wrote the obvious truth that I have taken as the title of this article, but I do know it has provided sustenance to my soul for many years. Because it is true: grass, like everything that is great and important in this world, grows at night, in silence, without anyone seeing it grow. And silence harmonizes perfectly with kindness and goodness, just as stupidity is always accompanied by noise and bright lights.

The great plague of the modern world (and we who write in newspapers are prime movers in the phenomenon) is that, as Søren Kierkegaard says, only fools get to use loudspeakers. The idiot of the moment gets married or divorced, dyes his or her hair green, creates (miracle of miracles!) a line of jeans for girls with holes in the knees, and there they all are: every magazine under the sun reporting the marvelous accomplishment. But if, on the other hand, you "only" love, "only" work, "only" think and study, "only" try to be decent, you can kill yourself doing all these trivial things and you will never make the headlines. The most minor criminal will be more important than you. Which is why those of us alive today are forever doomed to see reality as if through a distorting mirror.

The fact that in the United States there are hundreds of thousands of surgeons dedicating heart and soul to their patients will never make the news. But God help them if even one of them makes a mistake in a diagnosis or when he or she is in the operating theater: in no time at all, all of them will stand accused of butchery.

The heroism of the thousands of priests and ministers who struggle every day to spread their faith in God and to serve their brothers and sisters humbly will never be celebrated in any poem. But let just one of them get up in the pulpit one day with a stomachache and make a couple of foolish remarks, and you will see how every television station in the country broadcasts the story.

I could carry on like this with all the professions. I could also add that even when someone does pay some attention, it is only the most spectacular aspects of good that get noticed. I have no idea if Joan of Arc was a good daughter or a good sister, or whether she loved her family or was generous with her friends. The only thing I have heard is that one day she had a sudden attack of fervor and picked up a sword. And the truth of the matter is that it is a good deal more heroic to love for twenty-five years than it is to wield a sword for no matter how long.

There are times you can only laugh. You spend your whole life trying to write well, producing tons of pages, giving up thousands of little pleasures in order to stay tied to your computer (the modern-day equivalent of the torture rack)—and only a few dozen people even realize! But one day you go on television and talk nonsense for three minutes (for you can do nothing else in that atmosphere of spotlights and madness), and for the next month you are continually meeting friends who say that they saw you on TV and who even think the more of you for having achieved the wonderful success of getting your face onto the shining little box!

Yes, here we are in the information society, the society that informs us about everything except what is most important. Here we are, living in times when we will never know if people love, hope, work, and build, but we will be told every detail of the story the day someone bites a dog.

My feeling is that here we have one of the fundamental reasons for the bitterness that has invaded humanity today: the fact that we are shown only evil and that only stupidity seems to triumph.

This is not the fault of the media: from the very dawn of humanity, fools have always made a lot of noise. Just as a hundred violent troublemakers can make life a misery for thirty million peace-loving folk, in the same way a dozen miserable half-wits can make a complete mess of something that the best minds have taken centuries to construct.

In the face of this, all we can do is smile, laughing a bit at our human condition and at the broad strand of foolishness that is in every one of us. Smile, look at ourselves in the mirror, stick out our tongues at the foolishness of others and at our own . . . and keep working.

Because the great truth is this: all the nonsense in the world will never be able to prevent the grass growing at night—as long as the grass keeps growing quietly, without drawing attention to itself, and does not fall prey to the temptations of the lights and the noise.

Plato put it much better: "Nothing of what happens is bad for the good man," he says. Pain can trap us but not poison us. Injustice can assault us but not violate us. Frivolity can spit at us but not drown us. Only our own cowardice can lead us into disheartenment and, by so doing, corrupt us totally.

We attribute a quite disproportionate importance to evil. We devote the best of our hours to complaining about it or fighting it. And then we hardly have any time left to build what is good.

Graham Greene said that the famous station of the cross that is usually called "Jesus comforts the pious women" should be entitled "Jesus scolds the whining women." For could not those who seem to feel such pity for the suffering Christ do something more for him than simply cry? The novelist goes on, savagely, "Tears are only good for watering cabbages." I would add, "And they don't even water them very well."

It is true: there are too many whiners in the world and not enough workers. And tears are bad if they serve only to cloud the vision and shackle the hands.

Not a single tear, then! My eyes, when they are clear, know, even if they might not see, that in the blackness of the world millions of souls are growing during the night, silent and humble, striving and intense. They do not shout; they love. They are not famous, but they are alive. They do not appear in the newspapers, but it is they who keep the world going. On the surface of the planet are millions of flowers that nobody will ever see, that will grow and die without having been "useful," but that are proud of simply having lived and been beautiful. Because, as a poet once said—talking about roses—"What does death matter when one has lived, and lived so fully!"

How many battles have you lost, my boy?

The letter you sent me today, my boy, has distressed me greatly. You come across as so sure of yourself; you seem so pleased "to have matured"! I swear to you that I trembled when I noticed the disdainful way in which you talk of the years of your youth, your dreams, those ideals that, you say, "were beautiful, certainly, but completely unrealistic." You tell me that now you have adapted yourself to real life and that, as a result, you are a success. You have a reputation, a good house, a certain amount of money saved, a family.... You display all these things as if they were jewels on the neck of a fine lady. The only thing is that in the midst of so much pride, you let slip a tiny flash of nostalgia when you admit that "those ridiculous dreams were beautiful, at least."

Your letter reminds me of an old text written by Albert Schweitzer, one that has been in my mind for twenty years. I think you should learn it by heart, for it could be your last hope of salvation:

> What we have commonly come to regard as maturity in people is, in reality, a resigned common sense. Little by little, a person abandons the ideas and convictions that were dearest to them in their youth, and conforms to the model imposed by others. One used to believe in the

victory of truth, but not any more. One used to believe in humanity, but believes no longer. One used to believe in goodness, but no longer. One fought for justice, and now has stopped fighting. One used to trust in the power of kindness and the peace of the spirit, but not any more. One was once capable of great enthusiasm; not any more. To better navigate the perils and storms of life, one has had to lighten the boat, to dump overboard whatever cargo did not seem absolutely vital. And it turns out that one has thrown away the provisions and the water supply. So now, although the boat is lighter and more agile, one dies of hunger and thirst.

I read these words when I was little more than a boy, and they have stayed with me ever since. For I have seen hundreds of lives that mirrored them exactly.

Is growing up really such a terrible thing? Is life simply a matter of getting rid of things? Is what we call "maturity" nearly always just a matter of growing old, becoming resigned, joining the regiments of mediocrity?

Before you display such pride, my friend, I would like you to look over this list of six battles and ask yourself which of them you have lost. Whatever humanity remains in you will be clear as a result, of that I am convinced.

The first battle is fought on the field of the love of truth. It is usually the first to be lost. During your student years, you swear to live with the truth as your guide. But you soon discover how, on this earth, lies are more use and more profitable than truth; that with the truth you get nowhere, and that, as the saying goes, even though lies have short legs, put a liar in a car and he or she moves forward just fine. You look around and see how the people who get ahead are the ones who kowtow and suck up to others. And one fine day you too, my boy, you smile, you ditch your principles, you hold the doors open, you let them walk over you, you throw the uncomfortable truth overboard. That day, my boy, you suffer your first defeat, and you take the first step away from your own soul.

The second battle takes place on the ground of trust. We start out in life thinking that people are good. Who would want to deceive us? If we are nobody's enemy, how could anybody be ours? And that is when we take our first tumble. Someone disappoints us, perhaps even plays a dirty trick on us, and our soul unravels, precisely because we cannot understand what has happened. Our wounded soul swings from one extreme to the other. People are evil, we decide. We put up barbed wire around the castle of our spirit, install a drawbridge on the crossing to our soul, make sure there is no way to our heart without a passport. A soul bristling with knives is the second defeat.

The third is more serious, because it happens in the world of ideals. You are no longer sure about people, but you still believe in the great causes of your youth: work, faith, family, a set of political ideals. You enlist under these flags. People may fail you, but not these causes. But you soon see that it is not necessarily the best flags that win, that demagogy is more "effective" than truth, and that, very often, beneath a great flag there is an even greater idiot. You discover that the world does not value the quality of the flags, but their success. And who does not prefer a bad winning cause to a beaten good one? On that day another piece of your soul breaks off and starts to rot.

The fourth battle is the most romantic. We believe in justice, so righteous indignation swells within us. We shout. Shouting is easy—it fills our mouths, it gives the impression that we are fighting. Then we discover that shouting does not change the world, and that if you want to be on the side of the dispossessed, you have to give up your possessions. And one day we discover that absolute justice is impossible, and we start to turn a blind eye to little injustices, and then to more serious abuses. That is the day we are defeated in the fourth battle.

We still believe in peace. We think that a bad person can be saved, that love and reason will be enough. But very soon our soul begins to bristle, we start to become wary of being soft, we decide that certain people can be talked to but others cannot. It will not be long before we decide to "impose" our violent peace by righteous coercion. That is the fifth defeat. Is anything yet left of our youth?

We still have a few sparks of enthusiasm, faint hopes that gleam when we read a book or see a film. But one day we call them "illusions," one day we tell ourselves that "nothing can be done about it," that "that's the way of the world," that "humanity is a sad case."

Once this sixth battle of enthusiasm has been lost, a person only has two choices: you can either kid yourself by believing that you have been successful, and use pleasure and money to paper over the gaps in your soul where hope once lived, or you can hold on to something of your heart and see clearly that the boat is adrift and that we are hungry and empty, without the ballast of our illusions, soulless.

I would like to think, my friend, as you write to me today, that something of this anxiety nags at you yet. And that you still have enough courage to ask yourself which of these battles you have lost, my boy.

A dollar for the fruit

A few days ago I was having lunch with a family of friends, and just as we were about to sit down at the table, the mother realized she had forgotten to buy the fruit. So she turned to her fourteen-year-old son and said, "Joe, a dollar for the fruit." The look on my face must have been a real poem, for the woman immediately explained how in their house everything worked on pocket money; that the children did not do any jobs for the common good unless they were "bribed" beforehand: a dime to go down and get the newspaper, a quarter to go to the fruit shop across the street to buy the fruit she had forgotten.

And as the look of amazement on my face was still getting bigger and bigger, the children told me that this is the system that everyone uses nowadays, at least in their social circle and among their friends. They had to swear to me they were not lying, for I just could not believe my ears. And let me just tell you that I still cannot believe them, for if this is true, the funeral bells are ringing for humanity. Has money penetrated so far into the heart of that least selfish of institutions, the family?

I suppose that the world will come to an end before we ever agree on the role of money in human affairs. For we have been born and we live so immersed in money (or with the dream of having it) that it is as if it is the very air we breathe.

The Spanish language is full of proverbs that set money up to be something wonderful: "Whether it belongs to you or not, without money do not go to your cot," and "Money should be your hero, all else is zero, zero, zero," and "Sweeter than honey, money," and "The penny never betrays the thief."

Even the most intelligent thinkers kneel before St. Money. Miguel de Cervantes, the author of *Don Quixote*, assures us that "good foundations make for a good building, and the best foundation is money." And Francisco Quevedo, the sixteenth-century poet, says that "to step out in the direction of money is never wasted effort." Pedro Calderón de la Barca, another important writer, tells us, "Gold is the key that opens the most heavily guarded gate." The quotes are endless. And they are endlessly sad.

It is my belief that while it is true that people who live in poverty should spend their lives fighting against it, it is no less true that the ultimate freedom of which St. Teresa of Avila spoke can also exist, that state in which "wanting nothing, one has everything." Or that other freedom of which Ludwig van Beethoven spoke, from the saintly perspective of his genius: "I do not need money. Even though I were in utter poverty, I would not shackle my artistic freedom for all the wealth in the world."

But leaving to one side for the moment the role money plays in our struggles, how can one not tremble at the thought that it has invaded our homes: that a mother should pay one of her children for making his own bed; that another one will not set the table unless he is given money to go to the cinema? That money should become the measuring stick of our feelings is something that to me stinks to high heaven.

I remember that when I left my friends' house I reflected for a long time on why this new, sad state of affairs should have come about. And I could only think of two possible reasons: either those children do not feel themselves to be truly part of their family, or they have been brought up to think that you only work if you get paid for it. I do not know which of the two notions is more depressing.

Reasons for Hope

Reasons for Hope

José Luis Martín Descalzo

Translated by David Gray

Fortress Press
Minneapolis

—◆—

Ediciones Sígueme
Salamanca

and their souls burn with impatience. But their wait is not an unbearable torment. Their expressions light up, but their eyes do not glaze over. Do you know why? Because they never ask themselves whether what will arrive at Christmas will be lovely or ugly, magnificent or horrible. They know that what is on its way is, without question, splendid. The only thing they do not know is what kind of splendid thing it is. Their wait is joyful because they are totally certain. Children know that they are loved. All they want to know is how that love will be expressed this year. That is why children live in the midst of happiness, while we flail about trying to reach it. Children are happy with a single sunbeam. It takes an entire sun, as Goldweitzer has written, to unfreeze the frozen heart of an adult.

Adults do not know how to wait. And what is more, we expect things we should not. That was the reason we did not understand God when he came. We expected him to bring power, and he brought poverty. We expected an anger that would destroy our enemies, and instead we got compassion. We expected mysterious revelations, and instead what arrived was a little flesh-and-blood creature who eventually managed to say "Mommy" and "Daddy."

The thing is—he must have been mad—God wanted us to love him. He knew quite well that we are not capable of loving something unless we can take it in our arms. And that we would probably be frightened by the Lord of hosts. We would probably admire the God of philosophers. But we would only love him if he came as a baby. That is why Christmas is such a disorienting, dizzying, overwhelming time, such a time of excess. That is why Christmas strips away the masks of self-importance with which we have disguised ourselves during our lives. Christmas comes to dissolve the pounds of fat and grease with which we have smeared and shrouded our childhoods.

Because—alleluia!—childhood is immortal. The child we once were can be pushed into a corner, gagged, chloroformed, but never killed. He or she is still there, inside us, locked away amid our titles and our credit cards, muzzled by our experience, but still alive. That child refuses to die; he or she shouts and kicks inside us. The flying splinters of love that occasionally still burst from us are those shouts and kicks. Fyodor Dostoyevsky wrote that "the man who has a lot of childhood memories is a man that is saved forever." And we too are saved to the extent that Christmas can bring back to life the child we once were. This is a time to discover how mad we are, to realize that experience is just a figure who gives us a comb after we have gone bald, and it is a lot better to go around with your hair a mess than to be given a comb after it is too late. A time to discover that water is more valuable than money, that a poet is more use than a politician, that a child is more important than an emperor, that faith is the best lottery, that sitting in love around a fire should be one of the most solid stocks on the stock exchange.

That is the reason why, during this Christmas, when the world trembles with hunger and war, unemployment and nuclear weapons, Christmas and the infant God come to this earth of ours, this place that has almost forgotten the taste of hope. They come to awaken us from all this fear and to teach us to look at life with the same bright eyes we had years ago as we waited for Santa. I would like the world to become a great school once more, where we would all be sitting at our desks, with God as the teacher, and God would write the verb *love* on the blackboard. I often tell my friends the story of the great lesson that Georges Bernanos gave a group of schoolchildren one day: "Never forget that the only thing that keeps this hateful world going is the sweet love of saints, poets, and children. It is a love that has to struggle to survive but one that is always renewing itself. Stay faithful to the saints! Stay faithful to the poets! Stay faithful to childhood! And never grow up into adults!"

For if we could manage to do those three things, it would always be Christmas in the world. And our happiness would be so much vaster and stronger than our fears.

An insult to heaven

I do not think I will forget the sermon from midnight mass that Christmas Eve. The episode took place many years ago, when I was the chaplain of a girls' school. That night after dinner, I went to the chapel before mass was due to begin, and as I was getting myself ready, the sound of singing came to me. The girls had brought out a guitar and were having a sing-along after the fun of Christmas dinner. They sang happily and wholeheartedly, mixing religious songs with the latest tunes. Suddenly I heard the words of an old ballad that had become fashionable that year thanks to Argentinian singer Atahualpa Yupanqui. These were the words:

> *Does God remember the poor?*
> *Maybe he does, maybe he doesn't.*
> *One thing we know for sure though:*
> *It is at the table of the rich that he eats.*

I felt as if I had been struck by a whip. All of a sudden I saw how the sermon I had prepared flew out of my mind and the tremendous harangue I would preach a few minutes later came surging in. I think I cried as I delivered it, and the girls cried as they listened. I did not scold them for singing what they had. But I did roar at them that what they had sung was both an enormous lie and a terrible truth.

An enormous lie because all of us knew that the only time that God in the flesh ate in this world, he did not exactly do it at the table of the rich. Christmas night was proof of that. He was born in a cave. He shivered with cold. He had chosen the most dramatic poverty. He had remembered the poor to the point where he was born like them, worse than most of them.

But it was also a terrible truth, because the God we preached and lived was the very God who forgets the poor and who has very little to do with the Child of Bethlehem.

I know that the Peruvian Indians who composed this song saw God being represented by missionaries and bishops who, while they were personally poor, nevertheless when they came to preach in the villages, stayed in the houses of the rich, spoke and thought in the language of the rich, and had the rich sit in the front row of their churches. And it would have been the same if the song had been composed by the poor peasants of any other country in the world. How could they understand that perhaps God did not eat at the same table as those who represented him?

We smeared the name of God rather than preaching God's truth. We were falsifiers of God's Word rather than promoters of it.

But is it only the priests who are to blame? Each time Christmas comes around, I ask myself what their reaction would be if an Indian, an Asian, or an African who had never heard of Christ arrived in our cities in the days before Christmas. What would they think of Christ? Would they understand what we were celebrating and in whose honor we were gathering together? Would they not be more likely to think that the turkey, the Christmas candy, and the champagne were the real stars of the day? How could they imagine that our brightly lit streets, our businesses bursting with shoppers, our dazzling tables could have anything to do with the poverty of Bethlehem? Would they not wonder how we could possibly celebrate what was in its origins an explosion of generosity on the part of God toward us with such a crescendo of selfishness and waste?

I am not against people having a good time at Christmas (heaven forbid!), or the way children dream about it beforehand, or different members of the family exchanging embraces, festive tables, brightly lit houses. What I am saying is that when a Christmas dinner has abundance without love, it turns into just another slap-up meal. I am saying that when a gift stuns with its splendor but is given without affection, it becomes mere show. I am saying too that a family that goes to midnight mass after a dinner when the grandfather was made to eat alone in his room because the poor man is a bit gaga and last year was a bit out of line during dinner, that family is a bunch of charlatans.

For me, the happiness of children on Christmas is something sacred, and I would think long and hard before restricting it. But I wonder if a country that has millions of people unemployed can allow itself the luxury of spending the amazing sums of money that we spent last year on toys alone, particularly when you think that 90 percent of those toys will not make it to the end of January without getting broken. Just as I wonder if it is logical that a night out on New Year's Eve can cost twice the monthly pension of millions of elderly people.

Something is not right in a civilization that has turned Christmas into a period of gastronomic madness. And I cannot help feeling sad at the thought that the wise men who brought their gold, incense, and myrrh to Bethlehem would nowadays need to bring a jar of bicarbonate of soda to those of us who celebrate the festival in such a gluttonous manner. We need it to help us digest not only the turkey, but also the way in which we have completely forgotten the poverty that Bethlehem stands for.

The gypsy's miracle

After several years of study, a team of doctors from Lourdes has concluded that Delicia Cirolli's recovery from the osteosarcoma that she was suffering from is "scientifically inexplicable." The church, which is even slower than the doctors, may take fourteen years before using the word *miracle*.

I will not use it either to talk about osteosarcoma. But I will use it to talk about the human heart, a place where far greater miracles occur than in all the arms, legs, eyes, or cases of paralysis that ever happen to be cured.

There can be no doubt that in the story of Delicia in Lourdes, the most important episode took place in her heart. In 1975 she was an eleven-year-old girl from Sicily who came to Lourdes more at the wishes of her parents than at her own, for she knew nothing at all about the illness that had stiffened her leg and made it impossible for her to play. She had never heard the word *osteosarcoma*, and it was not until much later that she found out it was a type of cancer. She regarded her trip to Lourdes as just another family outing. Once she was there, she did not even remember to ask Our Lady to heal her.

"I saw so many sick people there," she told a French newspaper, "that it seemed ridiculous to pray for myself."

"So you did not pray to be cured?" the interviewer insisted.

"No," came the girl's candid reply, "I prayed for other people."

So the "scientifically inexplicable" recovery was made by someone who had not asked for it, by this girl who is a young woman now and who spends all her holidays in Lourdes working as a nurse and helping all those sick people who need it more than her. The miracle took place in her heart long before it happened in her leg.

This story, which I read today in a French newspaper, reminds me of another one that I have had stored away in my memory for the last quarter of a century. Since July 19, 1961, to be precise. On that day I happened to be in Lourdes at the same time as an international pilgrimage of gypsies. I have long since forgotten how they dressed and danced. But I have not forgotten the eyes of the old man whom I talked to as the evening drew in. From the stretcher where he lay dying bit by bit, a victim of stomach cancer, he told me that he too had not asked to be cured. "When I saw a group of paralyzed children out in the waiting area," he told me, "I thought that their miracle was more urgent than mine. They had not lived yet and I had, for too long. And miracles should take their turn and be fair. So I asked for my miracle to wait and for the children's miracle to be attended to first."

I have always believed that the true miracle is that of love. And I am amazed when I hear people saying that there are no longer any miracles in the world. I see so many of them every day! Heaps of people who love each other, men who struggle and sacrifice themselves for their families, people who help complete strangers and then disappear after they have given whatever assistance they could, women who cry because they think they have lost their faith, boys who struggle to overcome their passions. There could never be enough committees of doctors in the whole world to investigate so many invisible marvels!

And if I was not already convinced of this radiant reality, all I would need to do is read my mail of these past days to convince myself. It is strange: when all my friends are wondering if the last pope's visit will bear any fruit or if the whole thing might not just have ended like some magnificent fireworks display, I receive clear proof of the very fruits of which so many people doubt. Yesterday I had a letter from a businessman who for years has been running a small factory of just thirty employees and who at the moment is up to his neck in debt. He had decided to call in the receivers, for the company could not hold out any longer. But he has changed his mind as a result of the words that the pope spoke the other day, encouraging businesspeople not to take the easy way out by going for more cost-effective solutions during this crisis. He has decided to carry on and ruin himself if he has to, for even though his own ruin is probable, that of the thirty families that closing the factory would put onto the streets would be certain. He is going to continue, to keep going, and perhaps they might all survive.

Today I have received a long letter of confession from a single mother who for some weeks had been thinking about having an abortion. She is not going to. She trembled at the words of the pope. And she realized that all the shame and difficulties in the world are worth less than the life of her child.

I have also had a note today from a young man of twenty-nine who for years had felt attracted by the vocation of the priesthood but who had never quite made up his mind. He saw the pope presiding at an ordination ceremony and he asks me how he can go about following his calling.

Three stories that have come to my desk quite by chance. How many thousands of miracles like these might be happening all over the country?

I know perfectly well that we human beings can hurt each other simply by moving a finger. But I also know that we can help each other simply by smiling. Just think: many years have gone by, and the lesson of love that an old gypsy gave me in 1961 still flourishes in my soul.

The theory of the springboard

Alfred's visit has opened up, but also complicated, my afternoon. I let him talk on for nearly an hour without interruption, not because I agreed with everything he said, but because if I started to argue with him, debating each point on which I disagreed, he would not be able to express himself freely, nor would I completely understand his ideas, given that controversy clouds the minds of those who engage in it.

Alfred, who has just had a book published (*Twenty-two Clinical Histories*), wanted to give me a verbal summary of his line of thought. It is very simple: according to him, the key to all psychiatry (my friend is a doctor) is to bring patients to accept themselves as they are. Nobody can be cured or be happy if they keep on trying to be somebody else. Alfred interprets Hamlet's "to be or not to be" in a rather deep and special way: be what you are, be how you are, or do not be at all. People can improve themselves, but they can never be somebody else, with an entirely different set of virtues and defects. All of us have to fulfill ourselves as we are, accepting our own physical build, our particular social background, our intelligence, our way of being. That is the only ground we have to build upon. To dream of being tall, blond, and rich if we are short, dark, and poor is not only futile; it is also life-denying. It is not in our power, according to Alfred, to change the deepest parts of ourselves.

The sea has waves. A poplar stand gives poplars. The sea may or may not be happy with its waves. The poplar stand can only be happy giving poplars, not dreaming about producing waves. To reject oneself is the quickest route to failure. Only by accepting oneself can a person surpass him- or herself.

"Indeed," Alfred continues, "the big problem in a lot of families is that the members of the family do not accept each other as they are. The parents spend their whole time telling their children, 'You should do this, you should do that, you should be like your cousin Ernest....' Those children will never be able to love themselves. They will always feel that their parents love some ideal child in their heads, not the real child they actually had. Children want to be loved for what they are, just the way they are. They don't want to be merely tolerated. Some children get to the point where they feel that they have betrayed their parents' dreams and that they would be doing their parents a favor if they disappeared."

"Of course," says Alfred, meeting an objection that he reads in my eyes, "I am not talking about accepting the self in a purely resigned, passive way. I am talking about a kind of self-acceptance that includes a mechanism to fix the defects that each of us has—as far as possible, for there is not much we can do about them. Taking as a starting point the assumption that even with those defects it is possible to be happy and love and be loved."

Alfred left, and I have been turning his ideas over in my mind ever since. As I have already said, I agree with about 80 percent of them. The only thing that frightens me is that a position like that taken by Alfred could lead to passivity, that it could confuse acceptance with resignation and encourage laziness.

And I remember how I had been dazzled by similar ideas when I read Georges Bernanos's defense of the "cowardly saints." I will never forget that paragraph in *Dialogues with Carmelites* where he says, "God does not worry about whether we are brave or cowardly. What He wants is that, whether we be brave or cowardly, we throw ourselves into His arms like a deer pursued by hounds throws itself into the cold, black water." And it is true; God is probably the only being to treat each of us in exactly the way we need. He gives equal value to the love of the clever and the love of the stupid, the handsome and the ugly, the educated and the uneducated.

All this is true. And yet . . .

What Alfred could not have known was that when he came to see me, I was in the middle of my "Kazantzakis days." I am someone who is tremendously influenced by books, when I like them, of course. If a writer really speaks to me, he takes possession of me and, at least for a day, is the owner of my soul. And during these days, Nikos Kazantzakis has had the running of me.

And it turns out that Kazantzakis thinks exactly the opposite of my friend Alfred! The Greek novelist believes that the true homeland of the soul lies in the impossible, beyond one's own limits. His spiritual aim is to achieve the unachievable and to die in the struggle. What is important is not the happiness that one attains, but rather the happiness one aspires to; not the destination, but the effort of the journey. "Have faith in the human soul," one of his characters says, "and whatever you do, don't listen to the voice of caution, for the human soul is capable of the impossible," and "Go further than you are able to" is his advice to those who would follow him.

Perhaps there are different kinds of people, some who should be happy with what they have and others who will only be happy struggling to surpass their own limits. That is what Kazantzakis says: "There are three types of men, and three types of prayers. One type says to God: 'Stretch me, God; if not, I will rot.' Another type prays: 'Do not stretch me too greatly God, or I will break.' And others say: 'Stretch me as much as you will, God, even though I break.' This last is my prayer."

Mine too. At least it was during my youth. Now I struggle for it to remain so.

Or perhaps there is a synthesis. My theory of the spring-board might be useful here. Reality (my body, my life, my circumstances) is not an armchair for me to lie back in, but rather a springboard from which to jump. I accept myself as I am. I know that I will not jump if I do not take my position on the springboard; I know that I will jump that much better if I get a good footing on the wood. But at the same time I know that reality is there to be surpassed, that it is there for us to launch ourselves from.

Or perhaps the best way would be to apply Alfred's theory to other people (accepting them as they are) and to apply Kazant-zakis's theory to myself (not being satisfied with what I have been or with what I am, but rather spending my life springing toward what I will be).

No, I am not one of those people who dies of thirst dreaming of a golden orange when he has an ordinary little orange in his hand ready to be eaten. But neither am I one of those who forgets his dream of a whole orchard of golden orange trees as he is biting into his ordinary little orange.

The terrorist did not sleep last night

I do not think that I have ever spoken personally to Joseph A. Gurriaran, in spite of the fact that he is also a journalist, though he works for a different paper. But here in my notebook I would like publicly to state my growing admiration for him.

You will probably remember the dramatic story that put him on the front pages of the papers some months ago: At 9:35 on the evening of December 29, he was waiting for his wife at the entrance to a cinema, where they were going to see a Woody Allen film. Quite suddenly, just a few yards away, a bomb exploded in front of the offices of an airline company, right in the middle of the peaceful crowd that was going in and out of the cinemas. The journalist ran to a phone box to phone his paper, but no sooner had he lifted the receiver than another bomb went off practically at his feet and very nearly killed him. In the following days nobody in the media thought he had the slightest chance of surviving.

But our colleague had a tremendous will to live, and after the hell of seven operations in the space of five months, long and painful physiotherapy sessions, and many months in a wheelchair, he slowly and gratefully started to return to life.

But his biggest problem was that the bomb had filled his soul with questions. It is easier for a person to live with his legs paralyzed than with a load of unanswered questions. What was the reason for those bombs, which had seemed to beat every record for absurdity? A group of Armenians, in protest against a genocide that the Turks had committed against their people seventy years ago, and in reprisal for an attack that had been carried out against one of their group in Switzerland, decided to plant a bomb right in our city and take the lives of people who did not have the slightest idea of where Armenia was.

All terrorism is absurd, but this attack was doubly so. And Gurriaran was consumed with the need to find out what reasons, what clichés, or what madness could bring a man to travel to our country with several bombs and plant them in a public street used by people who know absolutely nothing about the cause that the traveler wants to serve.

For that reason, just as soon as he could stand with the help of crutches, the journalist went off to Lebanon with the idea of interviewing, if possible, the people who had planted the bombs. He found them. And I must say that the conversation that he had with them makes one of the most moving pages I have ever read.

"Your visit," the terrorist told him, "has affected me badly. I couldn't sleep at all last night. I feel terrible; this is really hard. If you hated us, it would be a lot easier . . . but like this, it's ghastly."

It is ghastly, all right. The chief of the group had started in a more abstract vein, explaining to the journalist that they know when they plant a bomb there might be innocent victims. But this is like a war in which some deaths are inevitable, even though they have nothing to do with the conflict. He was left without an answer, however, when the journalist put it to him that no matter how you looked at it, the problems between Turks and Armenians did not seem to have much to do with our city.

But terrorism would not exist if it tried to be logical. Logic was the only remotely human quality war had left to it, and terrorism has removed it. Terrorism is the ultimate corruption.

Or does terrorism still have some trace of humanity after all? Perhaps that nineteen-year-old boy who trembles at the sight of his victim's suffering is that trace. In one sense, up to now war had been a fairly clean business: the people you killed were always, or almost always, strangers. When you fire an artillery piece or a torpedo, you do not know whether the people you are killing are fathers or not, you have not seen beforehand the photographs of their children, you do not have to think about what you are destroying. You can even think that it is not men you are killing, but enemies. And you can do all this, after a couple of shots of brandy, without feeling much remorse.

But how is it possible to explain the terrorist who kills someone whom he has followed and observed for weeks or months, someone whom he has watched leaving his house each morning to take his children to school, someone whom he has stood beside in the bar that he goes to each morning, having a beer? I wonder if terrorists can sleep when they remember his eyes or when they think about those little children without a father. Or perhaps terrorism is simply a drastic lack of imagination. A work by Alejandro Casona comes to mind, *The Fisherman's Boat*, which tells the story of a woman who orders a stranger's death but then falls in love with the dead man as she gets to know him little by little after his death through the things that he has left behind.

I wonder if evil, in all its forms, is not above all a form of blindness. The day before yesterday, two well-dressed youths held up a young widow at knifepoint and stole a few hundred dollars she had saved, with great difficulty, to do some repair work in her house. Will the attackers ever realize the high price that woman will have to pay for the two or three hits of heroin they will spend the money on: months cooking on a little portable stove, without ever being able to have a hot shower? Selfishness dazzles us and prevents us from seeing the person next to us. The oppressor is ignorant of the lives of those whom he oppresses. People with more than one job do not know what it is like for the family of jobless parents to sit down at table. The thoughtless seducer will never know the outer limits of loneliness to which he condemns his victims.

Perhaps hell or purgatory is quite simply the result of what we do. Like the hell that terrorist was going through, the boy who could not sleep when he realized that behind all the great, fine-sounding words in whose name he planted the bomb, all there is is a crippled, mutilated man, a man chained to crutches, a man who . . . does not even hate him.

Queen does not laugh

In his latest article, novelist Antonio Gala writes how he sometimes has the impression that his dog, Troyla, smiles at him the whole morning from a photograph that he keeps on his desk. Reading the article, I am green with envy. For I have spent the last six years trying to teach my cat, Queen, to smile, and I have to confess my total failure. When she looks at me out of her shining cat eyes, she will sometimes express surprise, admiration, astonishment, or curiosity. But nothing more. I have never seen a smile on her face. She does not smile when she comes out to greet me. There is no trace of a smile when I give her food. Even when she is playing, she has the serenity of the Sphinx. And I have finally to accept the idea that she is not human.

I say this because I have always thought that what distinguishes humans from animals is not the capacity for reason but the ability to smile. And if this is true, why do we laugh so little? Are we only human during those moments of our lives when a smile lights up our faces and refreshes our souls? Of course, we do not think concretely all the time. Our minds seem to float in outer space much of the time. But if we think as little as we laugh, I am afraid we make precious little use of our human qualities.

Worse still, sociologists tell us that laughter is an increasingly rare gift. The world, they say, is becoming more serious; boredom is on the increase.

Eça de Queiroz blamed civilization: "Humanity was saddened at its great civilization," he said. Is it not rather that we are saddened by our great lack of civilization? I greatly prefer Martin Grotjahn's thesis, when he says, "Humor belongs to the upper stages of human development." How can we say that the world is improving if we are gaining in the number of cars but losing in the amount of smiling we do? Are we better off having central heating and not having happiness? In *The Brothers Karamazov*, one of Dostoyevsky's characters shouts, "My friends, do not ask God for money, success, or power. Ask him for the only thing that matters: happiness." (I do worry about the distressing thought that someone reading this might claim that to have money, success, and power, or even one of them, is happiness enough.)

Of course, when I talk about laughter, I do not mean great roars of laughter. Fools laugh a lot and smile very little. The most generous souls tend not to laugh out loud very much at all, but a smile is rarely off their lips.

I am generally mistrustful of those who are sparing with their smiles. I think the great Nicaraguan poet Rubén Darío was right when he said, "In general, smiling people have healthy hearts." And he was right to include the words *in general*, because we would have to exclude the people who appear in toothpaste advertisements. As well as those who plan their smiles according to Dale Carnegie's recommendations.

Even more dangerous are those people who cannot take a joke, the ones who get annoyed when they or their ideas "are not taken seriously enough." A friend of mine, Bernardino Hernando (in a wonderful book called *The Mustard Seed*), puts forward the excellent idea that "weak people hide their fear and their weakness beneath a veneer of seriousness, while the strong overcome the same problems with humor." Exactly right. There is nothing so fundamentally insecure as a pompous man. And the person who laughs at himself or herself in the mirror each morning has little to fear.

Apart from that, I would say that it is hard to beat a writer with a sense of humor. What I do not like about second-rate revolutionaries is that they take themselves so terribly seriously. They think that the sourer their tone, the more important they sound. But surely a true revolutionary is someone who sows her ideas with a smile. At least in that way she has more chance of their taking root in people.

When I think back to my childhood, I realize that my mind has ditched nearly every single idea that was ever preached at me in a boring manner. Sitting through the classes and the lectures was bad enough; I certainly wasn't about to make the ideas my own. But one thing I will never forget are the talks that Fr. Angel Sagarminaga used to give us. He smiled as much as anyone who ever walked the planet. He would get to the seminary and start to talk about missions, and when he saw that our attention was beginning to stray, he would stop and tell a joke or start whistling some two-part tune. For me as a child, that whistling was as mysterious and as awesome as Niagara Falls. And although experts would probably have thought the whole business silly, the funny thing is that now every time I hear a whistle, whether it is made by a person, a train, or a bird, I cannot help thinking of the missions.

People like that make the planet a greater place. They sometimes even throw light on our faith. Bruce Marshall used to tell how, accustomed as a child to the seriousness of the Anglican service, he began to be attracted by Catholicism the day he dropped a coin in church and it rolled through a slit in the heating system. Rather than telling the other boys off for laughing, the priest joined in the laughter himself. A God who lets his people laugh in church, he thought at the time, must be pretty intelligent.

And now it is my turn to laugh at how all this started because my cat, Queen, does not smile. St. Francis apparently used to say that it is by no means certain animals do not go to heaven. I take comfort in the idea, for if they do, I am sure they laugh there. We will all laugh. Either heaven is a sea of laughter or it is not God's heaven.

All parents are foster parents

I am becoming more convinced that Charles Péguy was right when he said that "the great adventurers of our century are the family men." Quite so: four centuries ago, when a man felt as if his heart was ablaze, he left all behind, boarded an old galleon, sailed to America, crossed hills and mountain ranges, and discovered a new sea or conquered a new nation. Nowadays, that same man with the burning heart sets off on no less a conquest: he finds a woman, marries her, and dares to have a child. And to do this he needs to be every bit as brave as the old conquistador.

That is why my admiration for family men knows almost no bounds, and I cannot but laugh a little when I hear people going on about the "heroism" of celibacy. Any adult knows that renouncing one's sexuality is a lot easier than the majority of problems a human being must face. And living alone, though it can be bitter enough at times, is not excessively so if one manages to makes one's solitude fruitful. In any case, it requires infinitely less courage than living through the whole process of fatherhood or motherhood.

The problem is that, unfortunately, there are plenty of people in this world ready to have children, but not so many who are prepared to be parents.

Let me explain. I am writing this after reading and reflecting on a text by Françoise Dolto, the famous French psychiatrist, who writes, "Three seconds are enough for a man to engender a child. Being a parent is something quite different. Really, only foster parents exist. Any true parent has to adopt their child."

The idea is not a particularly new one. Friedrich Schiller proclaimed it in one of his romantic dramas: "It is not our flesh and the blood which make us parents and children. It is our hearts." And not long ago the author of an educational text dedicated his book to "all those who think they are parents just because they have brought children into the world."

God forbid that I be accused of not giving its rightful value to the miracle by which one being transmits his or her flesh and blood to another. Just yesterday I felt a tremor run through me when I met Polly, proudly showing off a tummy just starting to swell with the first signs of motherhood. But that does not stop my feeling that true parenthood cannot be reduced to the miracle of a few human cells coming together and fusing; in my view, true parenthood is founded above all on the long chain of love that begins long before a child is engendered and that in the case of a true mother or father never ends.

I have often wondered to myself, do I love my parents because I am their son, or am I their son because I love them? And did my parents love me because I was their son, or did they become my parents because they loved me?

These are two profound and wonderful questions, and I will not hide the fact that in both cases my answer inclines toward the second option: love is the source of everything, not a result of physiology. We are children and parents to the degree that we love. Which means that every parent-child relationship is the fruit not of some coincidence but of a love that has been freely chosen and which is constantly being reaffirmed.

In this sense it is true that all parents are foster parents. Physiological parenthood was just the start. True parenthood is molded by and built on the unremitting love of thousands of days and dozens of years.

I interpret many of the conflicts that take place between parents and their children in this light. Conflicts like these are a heartrending problem for millions of people nowadays, but they are by no means a new phenomenon. It is enough to look at the history of literature to see the many plays that have portrayed children fighting their fathers, starting with the brutal clash between Iphigenia and Agamemnon and culminating in the drama of the brothers Karamazov and their brutal father, a drama that Franz Kafka and Sigmund Freud would later elevate to the realm of the sublime.

But it would seem that current levels of "high tension" between parents and their children are a particularly modern phenomenon. Riccardo Lombardi puts the problem down to the fact that today's children are in a sense the grandchildren of their own parents, as if a whole generation had been lost. According to him, the distance nowadays between parents and their children is the same as there was fifty years ago between grandparents and their grandchildren.

My fear is that the real drama of the situation lies in the fact that just as the modern-day world has lived an "acceleration of history" (in the sense that lifestyles and ways of thinking have changed more in the course of the last century than they did in the preceding nineteen), it is also living an "acceleration of selfishness." The assertion of each individual's unique personality, together with the recovery of personal freedom, both of which are highly positive, do however have an extremely negative downside: a decline in our tolerance of people around us, including those who are dearest to us. I worry that we are paying too high a price for material progress: we are either loving less or loving worse.

Do I mean that in every conflict between parents and children there is a lack of love on the part of one or both of the parties? I would not say this is always true, for we should not forget the terrible mystery of human freedom; but I think it is the case 99 percent of the time.

And I will go further: where there is love, the conflict cannot last. I believe deeply what the Bible says: "Love is stronger than death." Parents who never stop adopting their child with their love will have a child who sooner or later will repay that love.

That is the reason why I so greatly admire those true parents who know that the job of parenting never ends. That is why what I like most about being a priest, and also a journalist, is that these professions allow me to be the father of so many souls. And that is also the reason why I am just a little bit jealous of all parents. Because I remember the words of Francis Bacon: "Children may increase life's cares, but with all their activity they ease the thought of death."

The injured leg

Bingo, a dog belonging to a neighbor of mine who is a keen hunter, came back lame from last Sunday's hunt after a wretched trap nearly destroyed his right front leg. And the poor animal, whom on other days in the elevator I have to restrain from jumping up and slobbering all over my face, today sits in the corner with his leg up and looks at me with sad eyes, as if trying to tell me the story of his tragedy. But as soon as we get to the ground floor and the door of the lift opens, Bingo goes running out to his friends, the children, as if he has suddenly forgotten all about his problem, his right leg in the air, contorting himself in the strangest ways on his three good legs. It is as if he has suddenly become a clown and is deliberately making a joke out of his farcical lopsided walk. He runs and jumps without ever letting his injured leg touch the ground. You would think that he had only had three legs all his life.

I watch with astonishment and admiration and think to myself that Bingo is a good deal more intelligent than we human beings are. For I know hundreds of people who, when they are hurt in some way, spend months and months putting their weight on the part that has been hurt, as if they could not walk any other way. I remember John, who missed out on a promotion and who from that day on could no longer bear to do the job that until then had kept him quite content. Instead of enjoying what he had, he spent his whole time picking at the wound of his missed promotion. I remember Rose, a woman whose husband had cheated on her and who from that day on just let herself go to seed. Instead of coming to terms with her tragedy, she allowed it to poison everything else in her life: the love of her children, the affections of her friends, a job she enjoyed. She spent her time feeling sorry for herself, going back over her husband's infidelity again and again, like one of those Hindu widows who throws herself on her husband's funeral pyre and burns along with him.

Yes, I know hundreds of human beings who go through life putting their weight on the leg that hurts them most. They could live perfectly well in the same way that Bingo runs, letting everything that is sound in themselves take the weight, but no, they prefer to spend their time complaining about what they have lost.

I am not making light of the suffering of my friends. I know very well just how cruelly reality can sometimes shake and slash at us. I remember those terrible lines of César Vallejo, in which he says, "There are blows in life so heavy. . . . I do not know! Blows that seem to come from the hatred of God himself, as if in the face of them the residue of all our suffering were lying stagnant in our souls. . . . I do not know!" Blows that do indeed seem to be "dark heralds sent by death."

But precisely because I know exactly just how cruel those blows can be, I know too that it is in moments such as these that one has to take hold of life with both hands, take reality on board without hesitating, and realize we have no right to be cowed by the blows or to give ourselves over to the pathetic pleasure of feeling sorry for ourselves.

Our human condition is to be maimed; nobody lives for very long without losing some dream or other. There are times when it seems as if fate is being especially cruel; today we lose a hand, tomorrow a hope, the next day one of the mainstays on which our very existence depended, or seemed to.

But the other great lesson of life is that human beings can always put up with at least twice as much as they thought they could. If they lose one wing, they learn to fly with the one they have left. If they lose both, they walk. If they are left without legs, they drag themselves along. If they cannot drag themselves along, they smile. If they do not have the strength to smile, they still have the ability to dream, which is another way of flying in hope.

Apart from that, life is mysterious. When one door closes— the very door that seemed to be just the right one for us—more often than not another door opens and proves more satisfying.

Let me tell a story about something that marked a turning point in my life. (And I do not tell it to set myself up as an example, but simply because my own life is the only one I know.) It happened twenty-five years ago now. A short time earlier, I had begun my little adventure as a novelist with a story (*God's Frontier*) that was surprisingly fortunate enough to win the Nadal Prize. It was written with all the innocence of youth, and amazingly, it caused a great stir. Nowadays it seems purer than pure, but at that time some people found it offensive. How could "that" have been written by a priest? I smile today when I reread the outraged reviews that were published in some of the religious journals.

But all the fuss alarmed certain of the church authorities. And when, faithful to my calling, I sent my second novel to the church censors, the bishop in question decided that the book was very good but that there were four words that should not appear in it: the word *José*, the word *Luis*, the word *Martín*, and the word *Descalzo*. It appeared that it could not go out under the name of a priest.

I was not bothered about launching the book without my name on it (although I was not particularly excited by the idea of having it as a kind of illegitimate child). What really distressed me was seeing how my vocation as a priest was being forced into conflict with my vocation as a writer. And I was not prepared to renounce either of them. I suffered because a sword was being plunged into the very core of my soul.

Around that time I read a piece of advice given by Georges Bernanos, to the effect that "all writing is torture." He reminded his readers that "the world outside can make you suffer, but only you can let it make you bitter."

That was when I came to the conclusion that if somebody closes a door to us, there is no point in smashing our heads against it. It is much better to look around to see if there are any other doors open nearby we can go through. That was the reason for my turning to journalism at that point, something I had never thought of doing. If I could not be a novelist, I would be a journalist and wait for the clerical world to mature.

I think that fortunate decision is the reason why I do not carry a load of resentment around with me today. Thanks to that decision, I feel fairly fulfilled; I talk to my readers every week through my columns, and now, some years later, I am once again dreaming about and even roughing out the occasional novel.

And if that door had been closed to me as well? I am sure that I would have found another one. Or yet another one. For the world is full of doors if you simply reject the cheap option of settling into the easy chair of resentment and shouting about how unfair the world is.

This is no big deal. Bingo was doing it today, walking on his three good legs.

The right to make mistakes

A woman friend of mine who is a doctor told me a moving story a few days ago. She has a wonderful job: she carries out preventive analysis of various illnesses in newly born babies, illnesses that if detected early enough can be cured, thus saving many lives and sparing a good deal of suffering in later life. What happened was that several years ago, on a day when she and her colleagues were overwhelmed with work, someone in her laboratory, presumably out of sheer exhaustion, made a mistake labeling test results. As a consequence some children were given treatments they did not need, and what is worse, one child who had every chance of developing a number of illnesses was pronounced healthy.

Months later the supposedly impossible happened. The child fell ill, and the treatment, because it was late, was much more painful and a good deal more dangerous. All because of a mistake in labeling. The doctors who worked in the laboratory suffered over that mistake as much, or almost as much, as the parents. But fortune was kind, and the little one survived.

A year later, the parents came to visit my friend. To complain about the mistake that had endangered the life of their baby boy? No, they came to let the doctor see how well the child was so that she would not keep on suffering for the mistake she had made.

My doctor friend became quite emotional as she was telling me the story. She said that while a lot of people would have held a lasting grudge for all the worry and the pain she or one of her colleagues had undoubtedly caused, those parents had discovered that making mistakes is part of the human condition, that doctors have the right to get tired just like anybody else, and when they are not a result of carelessness or laxness, a doctor's mistakes should be afforded the same degree of understanding as anybody else's.

I think this is a fine story, especially since it ends happily and the boy's life was saved. The situation would have been a million times more difficult if the child had died. And I have to admit that I sympathize with the doctor. We are right to expect total commitment from doctors, who hold human lives in their hands. But we are not being human when we fail to recognize that making mistakes is in our nature and that, even when they dedicate themselves heart and soul to their work, doctors will occasionally make mistakes.

I do not like the catchphrase that I have used as the title for this article; I do not think that human beings have "the right to make mistakes." We have no real right to mistakes. What we do have is the right to be understood when we make mistakes, to be accepted with all our faults, to be forgiven for our stupidity, to be recognized as human beings who will inevitably put our foot in it seven times a day and seventy times seven each year. I am afraid that for as long as this law is not universally recognized and applied, our world will be a hard place to live in.

I have never believed in Holy Intolerance, and I do not think that it has very much to do with Christianity. For me, Christianity aspires to the ideal but takes as its starting point an acceptance of human beings as they are. Christianity is always well provided with ample supplies of forgiveness ready for use.

I think that the degree to which we are understanding of others is a measure of how adult we are. Intolerance can be put up with in young people, or is at least understandable. For young people, everything is either good or evil. It is only later that we discover how much good is hidden away in the creases of evil. And the extent to which evil lurks in the crannies of good. We learn to forgive as we discover the degree to which we ourselves need to be forgiven. For that reason, an elderly person who harbors bitterness seems to me the least adult person you could find.

Life itself teaches us to forgive, and forgiving is the most difficult art there is. We begin by forgiving in a melodramatic fashion, savoring the pleasure of forgiving, without realizing that, as St. Augustine said, "forgiveness can be a most cruel thing" when we forgive "from above," from the "dignity" of the person who has been wronged. Later we find out that real forgiveness is the kind that we do not even notice, the kind that springs from our soul quite naturally, without any effort on our part.

That is why the phrase "I forgive but I do not forget" strikes me as so absurd. It is one thing to learn from our mistakes so that we do not make them again and quite another to spend our lives remembering other people's mistakes, luxuriating in the sweet taste of our forgiveness.

Perhaps I learned to forgive from a teacher I had as a very small boy, a little woman who had the fine habit of writing our bad marks in chalk and our good ones in ink. The bad marks disappeared as soon as we did our first sum on the board the next day, while the good ones stayed written up there permanently, like a happy memory.

I think that if we humans did the same—writing bad things on the blackboards of our souls and good things in our notebooks so that they could not be erased—we would eventually end up without any feelings of bitterness, and our hearts would burst with reasons for joy. They say that "the wolf loses his teeth, but not his memory." Fortunately, human beings are not wolves; we can be lovingly selective in our memories. When someone asks us to forgive them, we can nearly burst out laughing, for the simple reason that we had completely forgotten all about whatever the offense was. This is not a hard thing to do: once you look at yourself and see the tangle of faults that is part of you, you stop worrying about other people's. The person who has difficulty forgiving other people simply does not know him- or herself. "Life teaches us," Johann von Goethe said, "to be less demanding of others than of ourselves." In my opinion, people who disregard their own shortcomings but who never understand other people's simply do not live very long lives.

That is why I am so fond of that little-read encyclical by John Paul II, *Dives in Misericordia*. He makes the point that the substance of God is "rich in mercy," that God is an expert in the art of forgiveness. Because God sees the truth in its entirety and the infinitely tiny nature of our weaknesses. In one of his novels, Graham Greene says that "if we knew the ultimate reason for things, we would feel compassion for the very stars themselves." Fortunately, God knows those ultimate reasons, the terrible truth that of every hundred wrongs that we do, ninety-nine of them are committed by mistake, out of tiredness or because we cannot be bothered, and that perhaps only one of them is motivated by evil.

That is why I am also so fond of what the Talmud says: "God loves three kinds of people: those who are never angry, those who never give up their freedom, and those who do not bear a grudge." There is no doubt about it; God will forgive us "as we forgive others." Or rather, let us hope that he forgives us a lot more. Let us hope that one day God will show us the child's soul that all of us have, saved in spite of all the mistakes that we make labeling our diagnoses as we go through life.

The war of the smart folk

The other day, a friend of mine came up with a surprising theory about the world we live in. "What we need," he said, "is a war. A war between the smart folk and the not-so-smart folk. But it needs to be a war that, for the first time in history, the not-so-smart folk would win."

My friend watched in amusement as an expression of bewilderment spread across my face. Then he went on to explain that in this world of ours it is always the smart folk who win: the ones who discover some trick or other to get out of paying taxes, those who make a living without ever lifting a finger, the ones who ignore the law, and those who use politics to force themselves to the front and get ahead. The ones who consistently lose, on the other hand, are those of us who in our innocence pay and work religiously, who put in our hours and meet our obligations conscientiously, who spend all our lives at the bottom of the ladder because it is not our style to suck up to the boss.

My friend told me all this while he was still pondering a defeat he had suffered recently in the little war of the parking spaces. He had parked his car correctly, but then the usual dozen or so smart-aleck types had come along and, no doubt taking as their motto the old saying "If you're at the back, speed up," had left their cars in such a way that my friend had had to wait for over an hour before he could get his out. That was why he was roaring about a world in which a few hundred smart alecks end up having their own way, to the detriment of all the decent folk who do what they are supposed to do and who behave in a considerate manner toward other people.

My friend was quite right: perhaps the world is not going well precisely because of all those people who pride themselves on being intelligent when actually they are not even smart. The smart alecks and crafty types would not be particularly dangerous if their behavior were not so catching: for after you have been walked over a few times, it is difficult to resist the temptation of doing a bit of tramping yourself.

There are not all that many of these smart alecks about, but they are well spread around, and there is hardly a factory, a company, an office, or a block of apartments where there is not at least one of them.

Take the slacker, for example. What group of workers is without one of these professional sloths, the person who always has some reason to unload the work he should be doing onto other people? One of his aunts dies every month, one of his children has an operation every three. He always has some reason to get out of the way when the hard work needs to be done, and to make his bouts of flu and his coffee breaks last forever. He knows that if he does not do his work, somebody else will. And he even has a good laugh at the expense of the "donkeys" who take on the jobs that should really be his.

Then there is the system-beater, the one who always finds some way to get around paying taxes, making payments, or meeting her financial obligations. Instead of working to pay off her debts, she spends her time finding legal loopholes to wriggle out of them.

Another example is the professional climber, the one who always has the smooth smile ready, who knows what time the boss will be using the elevator, who manages to be in the corridor at exactly the right moment, who always has a lighter ready for the boss's cigarette. The one who spends more time thinking about tricks for getting ahead or ways of stabbing other people in the back than doing any worthwhile work.

Even in the religious field, you get the "heaven seekers." During the years of the Second Vatican Council, every day at the start of the sessions I noticed how an illustrious prelate, who predictably has since been much promoted, would often stand at the door the cardinals used. His sole aim was to smile to the cardinals, greet them, inquire about their gracious sister's migraine or their eminence's lumbago, in short, to practice what he called "the ministry of charity." "The ministry of charity," of course, was nothing other than "the climber at work," since he could have practiced charity in a lot of places but strangely had chosen to do so at the very door their eminences used.

All these "cheeky" and "smart" and "pushy" types would not be so dangerous if their tactics did not work on other people as well as they do. It has to be admitted that in the short term, their way of going about things pays off: the climbers climb, the ones who take advantage of other people get away with it, and the smoothies wheedle and insinuate themselves to great effect.

Only in the short term, of course, and fortunately, only on the surface. For there is nothing so hollow as one of these cheeky types. Sooner or later their masks fall off and they come crashing to the ground.

But it is true that at least for the moment, they seem to be winning the war of the world. And they push decent people in the direction of that perverse logic that says, "God commanded us to be brothers, not innocent country cousins." A lot of people who used to carry out their obligations conscientiously no longer do so, just so that people will stop laughing at them and thinking of them as if they were innocent country cousins. And when they stop being cousins, they end up not being brothers either.

Have you noticed how many of our traditional Spanish sayings seem to have been invented by the smart alecks? There are thousands of proverbs that encourage people to wake up and not to be too trusting. For instance, we say, "Turn into honey and the flies will eat you," and "Charity opens the door to the plague." Likewise, we hear time and again, "Give bread to somebody else's dog and you lose your bread and lose your dog," or "From outside comes the person who will throw you out of your house," or "Raise crows and they'll peck your eyes out." The list is endless.

The world will never work properly as long as notions like these predominate, as long as it is the smart folk and not the intelligent ones who have the upper hand, as long as the smart alecks win out over the ones who are truly smart, as long as we glorify the brass necks and the crooks (as happens so often in the theater), as long as parents keep telling their children how great it is to live without lifting a finger, and keep repeating the phrase "Don't get caught out—use your head."

That is the reason why I want to pay tribute in these pages to the "not-so-smart folk," the ones who take pride in doing a good day's work; all those people who are more concerned about their own consciences than about whether they might get walked over in the war of life, the ones who place more value on their own personal satisfaction than on worldly success. For we not-so-smart folk will never win any war. But fortunately, whether we win or not, we will have lived as true human beings.

The new slavery

"I doubt if all the philosophy in the world can succeed in suppressing slavery; it will at most change the name. I can well imagine forms of servitude worse than our own, because more insidious, whether they transform men into stupid, complacent machines, who believe themselves free just when they are most subjugated, or whether to the exclusion of leisure and pleasure essential to man they develop a passion for work as violent as the passion for war among barbarous races. To such bondage for the human mind and imagination I prefer even our avowed slavery."[1]

These words that Marguerite Yourcenar puts into the mouth of the Roman emperor Hadrian are quite simply the story of our present-day society. Is the world really any freer today than it was twenty centuries ago? Have we moved closer to freedom, or have we simply changed the form of our slavery? In the Rome of the Caesars, there were ninety-five slaves for every five men who considered themselves to be free. Is the number of people who are genuinely in control of their own lives any higher today?

1. M. Yourcenar, *Memoirs of Hadrian* (London: Penguin Books, 2000), 104.

I do not want to give pessimistic answers to these questions. I am convinced that the world is progressing (in spite of all its setbacks). But I cannot help noticing that it is progressing very slowly and that even if the whips and ankle shackles have disappeared nowadays, human beings are still enslaved in more ways than they imagine. And of course, it is a lot better to be aware that one is a slave than to turn into a stupid, self-satisfied machine, convinced of its freedom in the midst of its slavery.

A slave is someone who is chained to his or her own freedom without knowing what to do with it. For freedom is not a virtue in and of itself; it is an empty space in which to build. Which means that getting our freedom is really just the start of something. It is no good being free to think if we do not bother to think at all, being free to express our opinions if the only opinions we have are about football teams, being free to build our lives if we just waste them in routine.

A slave is someone who is restricted by a lack of education or someone who spends his whole life in a job he does not love. Which means that half of humanity nowadays lives in slavery. What is the point of an illiterate person learning to read if she only reads comics? How can someone who regards his job merely as a way of getting through the day ever come to love it? What is the difference between a slave and the person who goes off to work in the morning simply because she is chained to her duty?

A slave is someone who is governed by fear or by his own bad habits. The person who only dares to think about what is in fashion when she dresses herself; the person who "absolutely has to" buy the latest gadgets, pictures, or curtains; the person who dies a thousand deaths from embarrassment if he does not have a car "appropriate to his standing," the person who goes to see the films or who watches the television series "that everyone watches."

A slave is someone who is a prisoner of his work, a person who destroys her health earning the very same money that she will later need to spend trying too late to recover her lost health; the person who struggles so hard to give his wife and children a good life that he forgets about finding time to give them his love and his company. A slave is someone who is used by her car rather than using it; a person who drags around with him like iron balls secured to his ankles the payment instalments on his house, their refrigerator, the home movie system, all those things he "could not live without," but because of which in fact he does not really live at all.

A slave is a man who is slave to a woman, or a woman who is slave to a man; a person who confuses marriage with a state of submission to her partner; the person who brings up his children not so that the children learn to enjoy their lives but so that the parents can enjoy their children. And slaves too are the children who confuse freedom with the right to make their parents suffer.

In other words, we are all slaves; we all have, at the very least, large areas of slavery in our souls. And what is worse, we are so used to these chains that we no longer notice them. "Nobody is more of a slave," said Goethe, "than the person who imagines himself to be free when he is not." Or as Seneca put it: "The most shameful form of slavery is voluntary slavery."

Freedom is too wonderful for us not to seek it out when it is in short supply, or for us to waste it when we find it. Really, few things are more of an uphill struggle than true freedom, which is a lot less comfortable than our ridiculous enslavements. I for one certainly do not think that being free is the ability to do whatever I want. Freedom can only be the possibility of doing those things that make me more of a person, that make me greater, more whole. Freedom squandered stupidly is not so much a form of enslavement as a sacrilege.

We can only be free in the cause of dignity, to love more or build better; never to lie looking up at the clouds or scratching our bellies. We can only be free if our souls are taut and aimed at something greater than ourselves. A lot of people say they would give up their lives for freedom, but not many are ready to use their freedom to build better lives.

Perhaps the greatest form of slavery in our century is what I call the two faces of unemployment: all the unemployed people who cannot find work even though they try, and all the people who have jobs but who do not feel themselves fulfilled in their work, who do not love their jobs. I always thank God for giving me an occupation I am passionate about, a job I would do even if I were not paid for it, even if I had to pay to do it. To be in my position is to be fortunate indeed.

But which of us will not eventually end up doing something if that is what we truly love and want to do? The other possibility, of course, is to love what you do. This is more difficult, but not impossible. For in the end any work is enriching for the man or woman who really puts his or her whole being into it. Those who are truly free in themselves make anything they do liberating.

And this is the most wonderful of all truths: your external liberties can be abused, but nobody can chain up a soul that is determined to be free. You can have your bread taken away, but not your dreams; your money, but not your hope or your courage; life can become an uphill struggle, but once you get to the top of the hill, nobody can take that away from you.

"Put your sword away"

A reader of these notes of mine sends me a card carrying an illustration of the "warrior Christ," which shows Jesus with a hard expression and with the barrel of a machine gun showing over his left shoulder. Under the picture my friend has written the words "Put your sword away," and he asks me to write some comments. But what comment could improve on the very words with which Christ condemned all violence forever?

I will just say that for me it would be completely impossible to pray to a Christ like that one (just as I cannot pray before many of the sickly cloying pictures of Christ as he appears on the old illustrated cards that people sometimes carry around), for the simple reason that I do not believe that he has very much to do with the Christ that the Gospels describe to us. Jesus lived in "a time of swords," violent years when people used to carry a *sica* with them wherever they went. (A *sica* is a curved dagger, which is the origin of the word *sicario*, meaning a hired assassin; it is also probably where the name *Iscariot* comes from.) Illustrious rabbis even proclaimed that the sica was the only thing that people were allowed to carry on Saturdays because "it formed part of men's normal dress." But Jesus was not, ever, in favor of swords. The early church knew this very well, discovering that while dying was a Christian activity, killing was not.

I do not, however, want to fall into the trap in which many antiwar people end up: taking exception only to "big time" violence, protesting only against the people who own the bombs, believing that the only way to build peace is to take part in certain demonstrations.

I am much more concerned about "our daily violence." The fact is that not only do all of us have a sword, but we live with it permanently drawn. Aggressiveness has come to rule our everyday lives. With the excuse that in this world "you either kick or get kicked," we all spend our time kicking out at what is around us. We talk about "violence in self-defense." But since we believe that "he who fires first gets to fire a second time," we go on the offensive before anybody has even planned to attack us.

Where does this violence come from? It is a weapon whose grip is selfishness, whose blade is our tongue, and which is powered by fear. We are aggressive because we are afraid, because we are unsure of ourselves, because we conceive of the existence of the person next to us as limiting for our small selves rather than as an opportunity for us to grow.

We are violent in the way we ration our smiles. Most of our contemporaries live all tensed up, as if they had swallowed their swords, as if they might wound themselves if they smile.

We are violent in our language. Have you noticed how aggressive we can be as we talk? Dictionaries are filled with swearwords. For instance, the word *whore* has no fewer than sixty synonyms.

We are violent in our tone. We continually load words with a double meaning by putting just a little more emphasis on certain vowels, so that apparently complimentary words praising people's intelligence or upstanding qualities can come to mean quite the opposite.

We use the sword even in our humor. An "innocent" smile almost always carries a hefty load of rock salt, irony, sarcasm, vinegar. To every ironic remark we always add "the sweet pleasure of hurting someone else" as a condiment.

We are aggressive, too, in our memories; we make a living licking old wounds. We have sanctified that hateful sentiment "I forgive but I do not forget."

We have even come to believe that intransigence can be a virtue. There are those who talk of "blessed intolerance," completely forgetting that wise old Christian saying "It is people's hearts that God wants, not their livers."

They say that some priests advise their counselees to go to a football game and insult the referee—to help them to put up with their wives better.

Joking apart, I believe that the world would change if we were all to take Jesus' advice and put away our weapons. As in the Gospel, our drawn swords are most likely to injure some poor Malchus, who was not even a soldier, but a poor servant. And second, we ourselves are likely to be covered in wounds, because violence is like Saturn, who devours above all his own children.

Ill from loneliness

I believe I have already mentioned on occasion that the most wonderful, and the most heartbreaking, consequence of writing a column is the correspondence I receive as a result. Wonderful, because week after week I see how people, or a lot of people, at least, are better than we think. All the affection, all the brotherly love that flows through their letters! The reason I say that it is also heartbreaking is that a lot of the correspondence I receive is suffused with loneliness. A good number of the people who write to me have nobody else to talk to, nobody else to pour out their souls to. They use me because they find something warming in these pages of mine. There are married people who tell me things that they cannot tell their spouse without getting a disdainful look or a "Don't start on about that again." Old people put things into their letters to me that their children or grandchildren should be hearing. People are ill with loneliness, the great curse of this splendid age of ours.

But of all these letters, the most moving ones are from adolescents or those who are in the first years of their youth. It is curious: the images we see on television or in discotheques seem to show an aggressive generation, one that is hungry for life and ready to try anything. But spend time with a lot of these kids, without saying anything, and you find it is all just a mask, that inside themselves they are lonely and often sad, that they shout and dance frenziedly to deceive themselves and escape from reality.

It has always been difficult being young, I think. But I fear that today it is more difficult than ever. We have brought our children up in a very particular way over the past few years, and all of a sudden we throw them into the reality of an enormously selfish world where they have neither the crutches that we were able to lean on as adolescents, nor any realistic prospect for developing themselves beyond the unlikely event of a stroke of luck. I remember that as I boy I had the urge to live life "in the raw," in the sense of living it with passion and enthusiasm. But now I see that it is today's generation who live "in the raw," for they live with all their wounds laid bare, without the protective skin provided by the love that our families gave us in our day.

I have on my desk, among others, letters from two young people that describe perfectly two versions of the loneliness I am talking about.

The first one is from a girl who has still not fully entered life. She is not yet covered with wounds. But she already knows the sensation of emptiness:

"At times," she says, "I have tried to work out the reasons for this feeling of unease that I have. Perhaps it is just the ridiculous adolescent crisis of an even more ridiculous adolescent? I don't know; all I see is this emptiness, this not knowing what is to become of me, this lack of aims, or at least, of compelling aims. I need something to make me fight and laugh and live, day by day. Perhaps what I need is a friend, boy or girl. I have never had any. People usually feel at ease with me, they tell me their secrets, they ask me for help; but I have never found anyone that I could really lean on. Perhaps I am a failure in one of the most important aspects of a human being: in friendship."

As you can see, the problem is not too serious yet; it is more or less the same sensation of loneliness that we all went through at the age of sixteen or eighteen and that simply forms part of the struggle of life. Every ripe fruit has been sour once upon a time. Every human being has groped blindly toward happiness at some time or other. All of us have lived the dramatic gap that exists between dreams and reality. The lucky ones take on reality with the same game spirit as they do their dreams. But there are not many of them. Oscar Wilde says that "we are all born kings, but very few of us conquer our kingdom. The rest live and die, like most kings do, in exile."

Can I be sure, dear Mary, that you will be one of the ones who manages to find and conquer your kingdom—with someone to keep you company if possible, but if not, then alone—and that you will not be content simply living off your regrets over what you have dreamed? Life has to be grasped with both hands, my friend. You have to show spirit in the fight and not allow yourself even to sound as if you are complaining. Friends will come, but they will be a lot slower in coming if what you are looking for is armchairs to rest in or drains to wash your regrets away. In the meantime, just keep being a friend to those who come to you. One day you will discover that the friendship that we offer as a support to others is worth more than the friendship that we beg as a support for ourselves.

I am more concerned about a letter that comes to me from up north. The letter is from a young man who is now in the darkest depths of loneliness, for he has just lost a love that was keeping him going.

"The last few months," he says, "have been a series of frustrations, disappointments, knocks, and cold shoulders. I have tried to kill myself twice and, luckily or unluckily (I am not sure which), both times somebody has stopped me. There were times I stayed true to my Christian faith and to the hope, perhaps futile, that 'tomorrow will be better than today.' But life just stayed the same. I am twenty years old. My hopes and ideals began to crack like a jar made of fine porcelain when I was still a child. The first pieces started to fall off the jar in my adolescence. And this year I am left only with the bitter tears that I cry in the solitude of my room. I hardly have the strength to keep on living this death that is life. They say that God squeezes, but he doesn't strangle. I am starting to feel the first symptoms of asphyxia."

Can I ask you, my friend, not to keep struggling in the hope that tomorrow might or will be better than today, but instead simply to start struggling for the simple reason that it is your duty as a man to live your life to the full, regardless of what it is like? How could we call ourselves men if we were only prepared to be men when we were happy, or to be more exact, when things turn out right for us? Do not cry: fight. Though you have lost a love, you have not lost all possibility of love forever. Forget yourself a little, and try to find ways to make other people happy. You will find a happiness there that nobody can take from you.

I have often thought of the despair that Adam must have felt when he saw the sun going down on the first day of his existence. He could not even have dreamed that it would return twelve hours later. He undoubtedly thought that it had gone forever. That from that time on he would always live in darkness. Would it have made his sadness easier to bear if he had torn his eyes out, given that the light had disappeared? He waited in the darkness. And the sun came back the next morning. It always comes back. And if it did not come back, we would invent fire, or electric light, or some other kind of light to keep on living. Because it is our duty as living beings and as humans. In any case, could we not all love each other a little more so as to drive off the stink of loneliness that hangs over the world? I am convinced that if we did, all of us together would make the sun of happiness come back more quickly.

Burning Judas

A priest friend of mine tells me that the young people in his parish have a "new" way to celebrate Easter. They have invented a ceremony in which they burn an effigy of Judas. My first reaction is that the ceremony has nothing new about it; that this has been a Good Friday custom in many parts of Europe for centuries. But I wonder if a ceremony like this can actually be considered Christian at all, and more to the point, if it really celebrates the resurrection of Christ. Is there not rather something dramatically pagan, and lamentably hypocritical, in those flames? Is this not simply a way of taking the easy way out by making Judas into a scapegoat, putting all the blame for Christ's death onto him, and in this way avoiding our portion of the blame and quieting the voices of our consciences, which reproach us for what we are doing?

The figure of Judas has attracted a lot of attention through the ages, but it would seem that it has become a veritable obsession in modern times. Rare is the year that some new play does not appear, or a novel, or an essay that tries to give an explanation of what is fundamentally inexplicable. The story of Judas is like a tragedy of which only the third act has come to light. We know how it ends; we know that he sold his Master and killed himself afterward. But we do not know the first two acts: who he was; what he was like; when and why his betrayal began; what he thought of Jesus; how well he knew him; if he ever knew or suspected that he was the Son of God; by what twisted process his love for Jesus, if he ever felt love for Him, became hate and revulsion. Nobody has ever answered these questions. They were left in the air when the gibbet brought the curtain down on his earthly existence.

But we refuse to accept this silence. We know very well that the story of Judas is not a mere anecdote half lost in history. There is something about his act of betrayal that speaks to us, that could perhaps shed light on our own destiny. Or that could darken it. That is why we continue to rummage around the story, not letting the man rest in his grave. We keep on searching. If we do not find what we are looking for, we invent something. And then we discover that nothing of what we have invented quite satisfies us, that no new invention is any better than the ones that preceded it. And so we collect Judases like butterflies, without the scalpel of our imagination getting any closer to penetrating the labyrinths of a soul that has no way in and no way out, a soul that eludes us, that will always elude us. Like the majority of artists who have never dared to represent his face and have preferred to paint him with his back to us or in shadowy profile, the evangelists have chosen to leave us contemplating a figure who is both vague and mysterious.

And our "collection" of Judases keeps on growing. The apocryphal evangelists started it with all their theories. In a fit of antifeminism, the so-called *Gospel of the Twelve Apostles* blames Judas's wife, whose greed presumably pushed her husband into betrayal. No less fanciful, though cleverer, the so-called *Arab Gospel of Childhood* looks for the reasons in Judas's childhood and makes him a playmate of Jesus, a wicked child who one day lost his temper and bit his little friend in exactly the same spot into which the spear would be thrust many years later. Among the apocryphal writers there is even a fundamentalist type, who in the manner of a latter-day extremist reinvents Judas as a kind of informant. According to this theory, Judas was a nephew of

Caiaphas who had been inserted into the company of the apostles with the sole purpose of keeping a close watch on Jesus and selling him when he became too dangerous. In the second century a so-called *Gospel of Judas* appeared. This was the forerunner of a more modern string of fantasies and invented a saintly Judas who knew beforehand that Jesus had to die, and therefore took upon himself, as a kind of homage to Christ, the ghastly role of traitor so that the Scriptures would be fulfilled.

But it is in modern times that the figure of Iscariot has caused the most disquiet. Almost nobody today accepts St. John's accusation, which sees greed as being the fundamental motive. Thousands of complicated explanations are put forward. Leonid Andreiev takes a psychiatric tack and blames everything on a physical deformity in Judas. According to him, Judas was a hunchback and quite disgustingly ugly. His whole life would have been a long story of rejection; and when someone, Jesus, stretched out the hand of friendship to him for the first time in his life, he bit it, used as he was to being constantly humiliated. Lanza del Vasto, on the other hand, depicts a highly rational, extremely intelligent Judas, the only person who truly understands the depths of Jesus' message but who, from the perspective of his loveless intelligence, cannot bear to see Jesus be "corrupted by compassion." Giuseppe Ricciotti and Romano Guardini defend the hypothesis of a love that evolved into hatred, a result of the feelings of rejection that mediocre folk develop toward saintly figures who are so obviously superior. Many others are returning to the figure of the "good Judas," which was first proposed by the ancient sect of the Cainites in the second century.

Yet the entrance to Judas's soul remains closed. In the end, both those who try to excuse him and those who burn him try to avoid the decisive question put by Romano Guardini: "Was Judas the only one to be tempted by the idea of betrayal? We should not speak of the traitor as someone distant and outside of ourselves. Judas forces us to look into our own hearts."

For that is the great truth: Iscariot is within us. We are all Judas. Who, in real life, has never betrayed the most cherished of truths, not once but thousands of times? Who has never violated the deepest of feelings and squandered away the sincerest of promises? Who has not compromised her principles and turned in the direction of some new sun that gives more heat? Who has not "adjusted" to some new situation? Who has not turned his back on his neighbor, that neighbor who is none other than Christ?

Actually, Judas has had and continues to have many more followers than Christ himself. Each of us has given more parts of our soul to him than to love.

Nor should we laugh at his thirty pieces of silver. Are the reasons for our betrayals worth any more than that miserable sum? What price for our little exercises in vanity, hatred, or revenge? Is a tiny portion of security or a promotion any more valuable?

I think it would be better not to burn Judas, for our souls could burn with him. Instead, let us go into the arena of politics, the arena of work, and the churches themselves and shout, "Judas!" from the door. Then we will see how all the people, how all of us turn our heads to look.

There was a child at the beginning of the twentieth century who felt deep sympathy for the traitorous disciple. That child had a better understanding. His name was Georges Bernanos, and he spent all his pocket money paying for masses to be said for the soul of Judas. And because he was afraid that the priests would refuse to say them if they knew who the masses were for, he used to say merely that they were for a "suffering soul."

Perhaps little Bernanos realized at some level that his masses were for all of humanity. For us.

The year that Christ died in the flames

I have never believed that Christ really died two thousand years ago. I have never been able to accept that his death should belong to a particular corner of history, that it should be pinned like some dried butterfly to such and such a day of such and such a month, all those many years ago. Theologians tell us that he is still dying, not only for us but through us; that, in the words of Paul, it is our duty to bring Christ's passion to fruition in our own flesh.

That is why this year for me will always be the year that Christ died in the flames. He died in the flesh of that boy who gave his life to save three strangers last Tuesday. His name is Al Temple (I say *is*, not *was*). A note in yesterday's edition of the newspaper said that Al "has honored our city." I would go a lot further: he has honored the human race; he has honored youth everywhere.

I have to confess that even though I did not know him, my eyes filled with tears when I saw his photograph. I looked at his long hair and thought of how he took off his leather jacket before he went bravely into the flames; of how he left his motorcycle there on the pavement, thinking that the lives of people in danger were worth infinitely more than a motorcycle. I cried because I was ashamed: how many times have I looked in disgust at boys like him as they came roaring down the street on their noisy motorcycles, bursting with the joy of their twenty years! How often have I dismissed them as empty, feeling myself threatened by their vitality! How could I have imagined that behind the long hair and the noise, one of them had a heart that was pure enough and big enough to risk his own life for three strangers? I swear most solemnly that I will never again speak ill of young people. A generation that can produce a single act like this one cannot be rotten, can in no sense be considered empty.

I hope that nobody will be shocked if on this Good Friday I make bold to speak of him almost in the same terms as I speak of Christ. I do not even know if Al was a believer. But how could someone who loved so much not be very close to Christ, whether he was aware of it or not? Last Tuesday Al celebrated the best Easter in our country, perhaps in the whole world.

It moves me to think that this boy's death reflects the three great qualities of the death of Christ: freedom, generosity, and salvation. The freedom of one who puts himself at risk without anyone pushing him or obliging him to. The generosity of one who does so not to save friends or acquaintances, but to help complete and utter strangers. The salvation of one who meets death at the very moment that three people escape from the flames—thanks to him. The fact that a human being can work this triple miracle gives the lie to Friedrich Nietzsche's claim that "man is the most heartless of the animals."

It is true that since that first Good Friday the world has become a much hotter place than we could have imagined. But it is not true that it is inhabited only by violence and the lust for power. Love is also with us. Love in freedom.

I wonder if all those people who go around shouting freedom realize that Good Friday is actually the great festival of freedom, as long as you understand that freedom does not so much mean that we should not be physically shackled as that we should not put shackles around our own hearts.

Jesus *is* freedom: no other human being practiced and lived freedom to the extent that he did. In life, he was a free spirit in the context of the customs and prejudices of his time. He was free before his family, before the powerful, before his enemies, and before his friends. Free in the face of the political parties and free in the dignity with which he treated women. His Sermon on the Mount is the ultimate expression of inner freedom. He came to free the sick from their illnesses and sinners from their sins. He preached his message while giving complete freedom of choice to his audience. He taught us to free ourselves from false gods and from false visions of what God is. He was so free, as Christian Duquoc has described, that "even his gestures and his acts seemed to be those of a creator."

He was free above all in his death. What a tremendous mistake it is to think that he died by accident! How shortsighted to imagine that he "was killed" by his enemies or that he was the victim of a set of unfortunate historical circumstances!

"There was never a freer act on earth than that death," Karl Adam claims. And one glance at the documents that recount the episode is enough to make us realize that Jesus walked to his death entirely knowingly, completely of his own free will, more determined and more aware than the boy who would imitate him twenty centuries later as he took off his leather jacket and entered the murderous flames.

A poet has written that Jesus entered death "like a person about to commit suicide walks into the sea." Like a person who is about to commit suicide, but who does not want to take his own life but rather wishes to give it to others.

That is why his whole life was one long Good Friday. That is why the *via crucis*, the way to Calvary, began the day he was born. "No one takes my life away from me," he said one day. "I give it up of my own free will. I have the right to give it up and I have the right to take it back" (paraphrasing John 10:18). And how impatient he was for "his hour" to come! "I have a baptism to receive, and how distressed I am until it is over!" he exclaimed on another occasion (paraphrasing Luke 12:50).

Did he not enjoy life? Would Al not have been happier today skiing or underwater fishing near his house on the beach?

Fortunately, human beings, all decent human beings, are a great deal more than just their own personal desires. Fortunately, the mystery that we call love exists, and we only really understand it when someone gives their life for it, like on that far-off Friday, or last Tuesday.

The fact is that today I feel both proud and ashamed to be human. Proud, because I have discovered once again that the human heart is vaster than the vastest continent; ashamed, because most of us spend our lives squashing it down to get it into a safe in case somebody tries to steal it.

What a wonderful thing, on the other hand, when someone imitates Christ and willingly dies for others! I remember now those two miraculously simple lines in which the medieval poet Gonzalo de Berceo described the death of Jesus: "And knowing that the time to leave was nigh, / he bowed his head and allowed himself to die." He did not die; he allowed himself to die, he who was Lord and King of life and death.

I try to imagine the death of that boy, after he had saved three people, when he knew he was trapped and felt the flames began to lick at his flesh. He must have been terrified. But he must also have realized that his death had not been in vain, that he would continue living in the three people whom he had rescued and who were now safe in the street outside. Perhaps he had a brief thought for the motorcycle that he had abandoned outside on the pavement, for the beer that he had left half finished in some bar. Perhaps he discovered that the best thing was just to bow his head to those ghastly flames. He certainly realized that he was not dying alone. He realized that his love for his neighbor had brought him to the same death as that man-God who two thousand years earlier had followed the same mad love for others, who had simply "bowed his head and allowed himself to die."

A field sown with future

I am risking a reprimand today. When I began this note-book some time ago, Antonio Alférez, the director of these Sunday pages, told me, "I don't want your Sunday article to be about religion; you have your Saturday column for that. On Sundays you can talk about the fish and the sea, but don't let too much of the priest come through."

I, like a good boy, have tried to obey. His request was logical: if people want sermons on Sundays, they can go to church. They do not have to find them when they open the pages of their newspaper. And though I love God more than anything else, I also love other things, and I believe that God is happy for me to write about things like love, life, and humanity; God was the one who made them, after all. It is true that there have been times when I could not stop the priest coming through, even though I kept him on as short a leash as I could, because I want everybody who loves life and goodness to feel at home in the pages of my notebook, even if they are not fortunate enough to believe in Christ, as I do.

But today I am going to risk getting told off: today is Easter Sunday, and I could not talk about the fish and the sea today, even if I wanted to. It is like when you come out of a tunnel and are dazzled by the light; no matter how hard you try, all you can see is that blinding light. Easter Sunday is like that for me, and it would be hypocritical of me to pretend otherwise. And I prefer to get told off rather than lie.

For the resurrection of Jesus is the root cause of all my happiness. All my hopes spring directly or indirectly from that source. And if you read between the lines of the earlier pages of this notebook, you will have no difficulty in coming to an important conclusion: this fellow believes in the resurrection. That is why he is not afraid of death.

That is why he is sure that the grass grows at night. That is why human baseness makes him suffer so much. I suppose that other people come to the same conclusion for different reasons. My reasons are that one far-off Sunday someone broke open a tomb and raised human dignity up high.

The problem with the resurrection of Jesus is that not even we Christians have given it the importance it deserves. We have demoted it to the category of a simple miracle or considered it to be the proof of other things, rather than having a wonderful absolute value in itself.

I remember how one Good Friday some years ago, my sister Mary was telling her youngest son, Xavier, who at the time was just six, how kind Jesus had been to people and how he had even died to save them. And she asked Xavier, "Would you be ready to die for Jesus?" Xavier, who, as you will see, was no fool, thought for a moment and then replied, very philosophically, "Hey, if I knew I was going to come back on Sunday, sure I would."

So as far as my nephew Xavier was concerned, just as for most Christians, the death of Jesus was simply a fleeting time-out in his life, which stopped one Friday and started again the following Sunday, as if nothing out of the ordinary had happened.

A resurrection such as this, understood as a simple return to life, would certainly be worthy of my admiration. But I could never make it the cornerstone of my existence. If, when Christ returned on Easter Sunday, He had simply taken up His life again as if He had never left it, the fact would have made little difference to the human condition and in no way would have made Christ the leader of a new humanity.

Let me explain. Christians usually think that the resurrection of Jesus was similar to the resurrection of Lazarus, when in fact there are essential differences between the two events. Lazarus's life was merely suspended by death. When he returned, his life after death was no different than his life before it. Both were earthly, neither was transcended, and both were destined to end in the blind alley of death. But Jesus' life before his death and his life after it were radically different: His life before his death was destined inevitably to end as it did, in death; but when he returned, death lay forever defeated at his feet. His life before His death was conditioned by time; his life after it was totally unconditioned. Jesus' death and his return were not like the sun that goes down in the evening and rises exactly the same the following morning. What returned on Sunday was a man-God infinitely greater in himself, an immortal conqueror who had won a "new" life for all of us. At Canaan he had changed the water into wine; in his tomb he changed the clear water of his life into the heady wine of his salvation.

If you understand all this, you will see why I as a Christian feel myself to be part of that wonderful affirmation of life and why all my hopes are based on the resurrection.

We humans think we are alive. But we are wrong: death has us chained up like bears in a circus attraction. The bears are allowed a few meters of slack to dance to the sound of the tambourines, but the chains are only ten feet long; forty, sixty, or eighty years when we are talking about human lives. Who does not feel on his ankle the touch of that chain that keeps us tied to death? Our human philosophies teach us to do our dances more or less well, but none of them breaks that chain. None of them breaks through the wall of death that closes off the blind alley of life.

Many years ago our brother Jesus taught us to break through walls when he moved aside the stone that blocked the entrance to his tomb. Thanks to him, we have somewhere to deposit our hopes over a much longer term than our banks would ever allow. (Although I should say that I do not believe in the resurrection out of some "need" for hope; I cherish my hope simply because the resurrection of Jesus is the root and the cornerstone of my soul. I would believe in it even if it was of no "practical" use.)

So have I done the right thing telling you about this? Would it not have been better, perhaps, to keep on talking about how beautiful the world is, as if I saw that as an absolute value in itself? Might the fact that I have come clean about this cornerstone of my vision of the world not perhaps distance those who do not share my faith? I would be sorry if that happened. I would also like to be a brother to those who do not believe. But I want to make one thing clear: even when I do not talk about it, my faith is at the heart of all my happiness. I cannot lie.

The bad guy in the film

Doctor Thomas Forman has discovered that the human body is getting more expensive, just like tomatoes and potatoes. According to his studies, the monetary value of the inorganic material of which we are made amounted to the petty sum of 98 cents in 1963. By 1969 it had gone up to $3.50. And thanks to recent price increases in a whole range of chemical products, we are now worth $5.60: more or less the price of one of the cheapest meals in an American fast-food restaurant.

Wise men tell us that our bodies apparently do not amount to much. Three-fourths is pure water. We do have some fats, but barely enough to fry a couple of eggs. And all the iron contained in our organism would hardly be enough to make a single nail.

As you can see, we are not worth much, even though an athlete's legs are insured for millions. Or some boxers are said to have fists of gold. Or some people are referred to as having bodies like cathedrals. Or a pound of flesh fetches a high price in the pleasure markets of the night. Five dollars in fact, if you weigh 160 pounds and are well fed. I can almost understand how people who do not believe much in life hardly give any value at all to an unborn child, whose body in monetary terms is worth a good deal less than a cup of coffee.

What strange conclusions we are led to by a philosophy that reduces everything to economics! Joaquín Antonio Peñalosa was right when he said that after centuries of believing humanity was the king of creation, materialism has come along and checkmated the king.

But I fear that the road to that checkmate was prepared beforehand by something that I do not know whether to call spiritual ingenuity or religious materialism. For I believe that within Christianity itself, a shortsighted asceticism has set the value of the human body at even less then Dr. Forman's five dollars.

I have never understood why so many preachers have the habit of talking about the human body as if it were the bad guy in the film. It would appear that the human soul is a respectable lady, full of good qualities, wedded (unfortunately for her) to a wretched body that she has to put with like people put up with a failed marriage. The soul apparently aspires constantly in the direction of God, while the body passes its time pulling the soul down toward the mud and the hay.

A widely read spiritual book of the past few decades refers to the human body, at least ten times, as treacherous and contrary. The soul should spend its time on guard against the body, reining it in, since apparently the body is "an enemy to the glory of God." We cannot even trust our own heart, and we should keep it bolted tight, given that "even though the flesh be dressed in silk, flesh it still remains."

I can understand the good intentions that are enshrined in these phrases, since at bottom what is being attacked is sexual deviancy rather than the flesh itself. But I fear that great oversight or, what is worse, Manichaeism lies behind all of them.

Perhaps this is the reason why a sizable percentage of Christians cannot really accept the incarnation of Christ. They think that Jesus was a "special man," one "with a human appearance" but one who did not completely inhabit such a despicable thing as the human body. Would anybody dare to say of Christ's adorable flesh that "the flesh remains" in the disrespectful sense?

The lack of faith felt by many believers in the resurrection of the flesh clearly has its roots in this. Rather than as a creedal doctrine, we almost regard it as a dirty trick. It is as if we thought that after we have gone through life putting up with our bodies in this world, it wouldn't be right that God should take the bad guy that was keeping us in chains up to heaven. As a result, there are preachers who, to get around the problem, invent a so-called spiritual flesh, which is neither fish nor fowl, neither body nor soul.

But actually Christ in the Gospels made it very clear that sin is not what goes in through people's mouths but what comes out of their interior. And he said that evil desires come from the soul, from our will. From which we can conclude that it is the soul that mistreats the body each time we sin.

It seems to me that all this is at the origin of the taboo vision that is sometimes put about regarding anything to do with the body and sexuality, as if one and the other were by nature bad and that the only way to purify them is to "give them a good dose of soul." So we abuse, insult, and revile our sacred companion in arms, that very flesh, which when it resuscitates will be resuscitated flesh, and not some kind of spiritual hybrid.

I think that we should begin by accepting that God did a fairly good job of creating us human beings. It is not as though he made a mistake brewing a cup of coffee, giving us a delicious soul but a sour body that we need to spend our lives pouring sugar into. He created freedom, it is true, and that inevitably has risks. But it is the body and the soul together that struggle to build the house of happiness.

Emilio Ferrari made the point in some rather rhetorical and slightly precious lines, but he expressed it well: "The body is not some miserable rag, surrendered to death as our ransom. It is the tool of our daily labor, our armor in the struggle."

It is true. We could not fulfill ourselves if we did not have a body. And we could certainly not be Christians without one. So really we should not only respect but positively revere this human flesh that God will make eternal.

I would like to tell a story now, one that years ago chilled me to the core. One day, as I was leaving a church where I had spoken about the resurrection of the flesh, a young man was waiting for me at the door. His eyes were on fire. "Do you really, truly believe what you have just preached?" he asked me. His words shook me, for they were as fiery as his eyes, and I realized that a good part of his life would depend on my answer. When I said that yes, for the church that was dogma and not just a metaphor, I saw him take a deep breath and saw the fire in eyes turn into a calm light. He told me that he had not been able to believe for ten years, since the day of his mother's burial. His mother had died while he was on a trip, and his father had delayed the funeral for a day so that he could get there in time. And when he had gone up to the coffin to see her just before it was closed, he hardly recognized her, for she had started to . . . The young man could not say the word. He stopped as if terrified on the edge of a precipice. "I could accept my mother's death," he said, "but not what was happening to that body that had given birth to me." This poured out of him at such a rate that he could hardly breathe. When he got his breath back, he added, "That is why it has never been enough for me to know that my mother's soul was immortal. I loved her body. I still love her body. I need to see it again the way it was before that moment." I said, "You will see it again." And I saw how his eyes relaxed, how joy swept through him, how ten years of anguish left him.

But that morning, the young man helped me more than I helped him. For I realized then that if we want to value our human body, we need to think of the sacred body that engendered us. And when I thought of that body, I understood with an irrevocable conviction that it "must" be true that all our sacred bodies will resuscitate.

The sweet kingdom

A few years before the end of his life, in a letter to a friend, Georges Bernanos wrote a sentence he would never have dared to set down in any of his books. His tone is almost sheepish, and the words are ones that I keep in my memory like a treasure: "When I die, tell the sweet kingdom of earth that I loved her a lot more than I have ever dared say."

That sentence portrays me also, with a terrible precision. And I, who have a lot fewer qualms than the great French writer, want to say so here, publicly, for I am terrified by the slanderous insinuation that we believers do not love this world, that we are so obsessed by the next one that we regard the dear, sweet, enthralling little kingdom of earth with a total lack of interest.

I know that in their efforts to glorify the wonder of what awaits us, for centuries Christian ascetics have disdained our home on earth or at least have seemed to do so. How many times has St. Teresa's famous phrase, the one in which she defines life in this world as "a bad night in a bad inn," been taken out of context, used and abused! There is in fact no hint of disdain in these words from *The Way to Perfection*, in which the saint from Avila, far from undervaluing the importance of time, encourages her nuns to put a good face on the sufferings and rigors of transitory things. What about all the other phrases of hers in which she calls her little convent of St. Joseph a "paradise"? Why are they much less quoted?

I remember how twenty years ago, the Jansenite priest whom I was then, my whole soul prickling with needles, nearly had a heart attack when he read the ever-so-slightly heretical poem that Jorge Guillén had written about Lazarus. The poet depicts a Lazarus who is disconcerted to find, when he comes back from the dead, that he almost prefers this little world to the vague existence that he had experienced in a death and a paradise that were in a way almost too big for him. He discovers that in this world he finds himself "happy, in his humble way." He knows that here "in this little lane" he is "the real Lazarus." He recognizes that "out there is where the kingdom is," on the other side. He admits that he wants to enjoy the sight of God. But he discovers that he would like the other world to be a lot like this one. He turns to God and begs, "If I were a dweller in your Glory, give me a place that is like Earth, with all its monotony and all, but with woods and close by the sea, its sands." He wonders with a kind of anguished humility if "when he undertakes the great journey again" he will have to leave behind any of the things that he loves so much in this life. And he prays that the Beatitudes will help him "to overcome adversity and become the man whom you have made, so human."

As I say, I remember how my little priest thought that this was very close to heresy, how anyone could reject the Great Glory and prefer it to be made up of lots of little minor glories.

I will confess that the priest I am today finds the idea a lot less heretical; in fact, at bottom he finds himself in brotherly sympathy with such a wish. I like the kingdom of this world. And this love does not reduce in the slightest my desire for the Great Kingdom, except that now I imagine it as a place less cold, one made up more of summers, woods, and sands. Would God be any the less in the midst of these marvels than among groups of delicate angels at play?

I have very often wondered if Christ liked this world, or if he wanted to return to his Father. And I always tell myself that, like so many lesser mystics after him, he was almost certainly torn between two loves: love for this earth and the people on it, whom he had made in his own image and likeness, and the great dazzling light of eternity. Certainly the fact that he had experienced the infinite happiness of eternal glory did not make the beauty of the sun setting over the lake at Gennesaret seem any the less.

And after all these thoughts, which the inquisitors would have no time for, my consolation is that the God who made us "so human" will not be too surprised that we aspire in our human way to a rather tawdry version of heaven.

Perhaps when we get up there, our souls will be expanded and we will discover pleasures that here we cannot even imagine. But as long as we are here, why should we not love this world that he made to suit us so perfectly? Not even the saints lived on a knife edge all the time. St. Teresa of Avila herself admitted that "any soul, no matter how perfect, has to have a pressure valve."

So then, whether it be a drain or a virtue, I will allow myself to feel enamored of this "sweet kingdom." I will reflect that if Christ took his humanness with him into eternity, I might be allowed to take a flowerpot from this world into the next life. For I know that even though one will never tire of the sight of God, during those times when I simply cannot be exalted, they might let me look at my flowerpot for a few centuries.

The virtues of *and*

I have long been amazed at the fondness humanity has for the word *or*. This *or* of ours constantly forces us to choose, to decide for one thing as opposed to another, to join one camp or another. Any American worthy of the name has to choose between rural life or city life, between football or baseball, be politically inclined toward the left or the right, enjoy summer or winter, prefer meat or fish. Would it not be possible instead to choose as a guiding principle the word *and*? Then you could opt for rural life and city life simultaneously, football and baseball, autumn and spring, a little of the left and a little of the right, or perhaps neither, a fish dish followed by a plate of meat, or perhaps a couple of eggs. It would seem not. A good person apparently has to give a daily demonstration of this attitude of either/or, this spiritual separatism, this intransigence, which has on occasion been called "holy intolerance," in a phrase reminiscent of the lines from a popular opera:

> *I proclaim myself a free thinker*
> *In a voice loud and clear.*
> *But woe betide anyone*
> *Who thinks different from me.*

I can only presume that I am very unpatriotic in this respect, for as it happens, I love that *and*. And the funny thing is that my preference has its roots in my studies of Catholic theology, which itself has a considerable reputation for intolerance.

I remember that while I was doing my theology courses, I was very struck by the way in which our doctrines will often get around a dilemma simply by leaping over it and demonstrating their truth through synthesis. We used to be asked, for example, if God was one or a trinity, if Christ was God or a man, if Mary was a virgin or a mother, if human beings were saved by their own efforts or purely through the grace of God, and so on. In all these cases, logic dictated that we had to choose one or the other option, since if one proposition was true, the other could not possibly be. That is, if Mary was a virgin, she could not be a mother; the nature of God was different than that of man; and human effort was quite distinct from divine grace. But then understanding would dawn, and you would see that the answer lay beyond human logic and that it was not necessary to choose between the propositions. God could be one and a trinity. Mary was a virgin and a mother at the same time. Christ is both man and God, and salvation comes from human effort and divine grace simultaneously.

I liked this way of approaching and resolving problems. For I had discovered that although there are things that are quite incompatible from the metaphysical point of view, many others, which we hurriedly take to be contradictory, are in fact, from an objective standpoint, perfectly compatible and combinable.

For example, I had long puzzled over a notice hanging above the door of one of the houses in the village where I lived as a child. The notice had been there since the time of the civil war and proclaimed the following: "Long live the law of Christ. Death to freedom." I did not understand. Why was I being forced to choose between the law of Christ and freedom? I loved both. And I was of the opinion that the law of Christ was the greatest of all possible freedoms and that there could be no contradiction between it and any true freedom.

Nor had I ever been convinced by the argument that since two and two make four, and never three and one-half, those who are in possession of "the truth" ought to be intolerant. First of all, because I had never felt myself to be in possession of the truth; in fact, what I aspire to with all my heart is for the truth to possess me. And second, because although it is true that two and two will never be three and one-half, it is also true that while four is the result of adding two and two, it is also the result of adding three and one, two and one-half and one and one-half, two and one and one, and a hundred other combinations—which proved to me that while there is only one truth, there are hundreds of different ways to get to it.

That is why I have always preferred to add rather than to divide, to go beyond rather than to choose, to share rather than to pigeonhole. When I was told I had to work with my hands and not with my knees, I would ask myself, "And why not with my hands and with my knees?" When I was asked to opt for law and order or justice, I always replied that one without the other is impossible, and that you cannot secure and preserve the latter without having the former. When people asked whether I preferred to be Christian or up to date, I used to cry that I loved being both and that I was not prepared to sacrifice being either.

Perhaps that is why I am so fond of St. Teresa, for in a century that was even more divisive than our own, she was a supporter of prayer and action, of the inner life and extraversion, of the ascetic disciplines and humanism, of freedom and obedience, of loving God and loving the world, of being critical of the errors of the church while caring deeply for the affairs of the church. Definitely, I have always been enthusiastic about people who were on the side of *and*.

I can only laugh when I think of that teacher I had in the seminary who held up his faith as a reason for detesting all modern inventions. Everything infringed on some item of doctrine. Perhaps that was why he died without allowing himself to be given a single medicinal shot, because he argued that "if God had wanted us to get shots, he would have made us with a little hole to have them in." Luckily, apart from being narrow-minded, he was also quite good fun, and he used to add (and please forgive the joke), "He already gave us all the holes we need."

Encouraging those who fail

I have always wondered why, in the traditional lists of works of mercy, the old catechisms did not include a fifteenth, "Encourage those who fail," something that should be uppermost in the minds of all parents at the time of exams. For if we cannot call on help of this sort in the midst of the kind of inner collapse that failing a lot of subjects brings about when we are eight, twelve, or fourteen, what is the point of living in the company of our fellow human beings?

We should have the greatest respect for the suffering of children, for their sense of frustration, for the bitterness that, especially in the best of them, can cast a dark cloud over the horizons of life.

I believe that a true parent, or a true teacher (for a teacher who does not act as a parent is not, in my view, a teacher at all), ought to be extremely demanding before examinations and extremely forgiving after them. Demanding, because children must be made to see that failing out of laziness or lack of interest is morally equivalent to robbing their parents and robbing society: they are effectively robbing the family and the community of everything they have invested over the course of the year.

The curious thing is that the parents who are the most permissive before the exams are the ones who are the least understanding after them, when this should be the time to encourage, not dishearten. It terrifies me to think of the huge number of children who will be getting held up in their lives these days thanks to a combination of a lack of commitment and study on their own part and the absence of help and stimulation from their parents.

For if it is robbery to fail a year at school, to throw your whole life away as a result is plain stupid.

So I believe that this is the time to explain to a lot of children, especially the brightest ones, that many geniuses slipped up in their studies at one time or another. That one subject failed is only dangerous when it becomes the first link in a whole chain of failed subjects.

To tell them, for example, that Nobel Prize winner Dr. Severo Ochoa failed medicine twice. Jaime Balmes, the philosopher, flunked math. Both Ramón Gómez de la Serna and Azorín (José Martínez Ruiz), notable Spanish writers, slipped up precisely in literature. Federico García Lorca's school record shows him as having once failed in the history of Spanish. And all of them ended up achieving great success in the very subjects in which they had once been weak. Because they did not allow themselves to get bogged down by the fact they had failed. Because they were able to turn that into an incentive to do better, in just the same way as when we trip, if we manage not to fall, we actually go much faster than if we had not tripped in the first place.

And it is above all important to explain to these children that the saying "Geniuses are born, not made" is the most ridiculous, and most dangerous, piece of nonsense ever invented by humanity. Of course a Wolfgang Mozart comes along every once in a while, but only one of every thousand child prodigies is ever really successful, and what usually happens is that genius is the result of constant everyday hard work.

I remember the example of Albert Einstein, one of the fathers of modern science. His biographers tell us that as a child he was exceptionally slow. At the age of three he still could not talk, only utter a few words that were so badly pronounced that his parents had become resigned to the idea of having a mentally handicapped child.

When he caught up at the age of six, his shyness made it seem as if he was still backward. "Boring little Daddy" his classmates called him. And later, during the years of his secondary studies, he almost never got higher than 70 percent. He was such an ordinary student that when he became a famous scientist, and journalists wanted to go back over the years of his youth, they found that none of his fellow students could remember anything about him.

Heaven forbid that anyone should think I am saying that children should not care about how they do in their exams. But I think I can say that they should not give the matter more importance than it deserves, that it is a proven fact that seven out of every ten children who come to the top of their class at school go on to do very ordinary things in life, and it is often the average children who one day show the greatest inner potential.

Personally, I admire determination and hard work more than genius or intelligence. The people who are successful in life are not the ones who have rays of light shining from their foreheads, but rather the ones who show grit and strength of will in what they do, who set up clear objectives for themselves and then work toward them without getting distracted. I fully agree with the phrase of George Bernard Shaw's that "genius is a long apprenticeship," or with what Joseph Joubert said: "Genius starts great works, but only hard work finishes them." Or with Ludwig van Beethoven, who put it in a catchier way: "Genius is composed of 2 percent talent and 98 percent work."

I remember that in the years when I was a teacher, I never got tired of writing on the board a mathematical formula that summed up in three numbers my view of the value of human beings. The formula was this: $1I \times 2C \times 10W = X$. Which translated into words meant that a human being is equal to his or her IQ multiplied by twice the circumstances of his or her life, multiplied by ten times the work he or she puts into achieving goals. From which it was possible to deduce that a genius of a child (10 for intelligence) who was extremely fortunate in his or her circumstances (10 for favorable circumstances all his life), but who was not very hardworking (2 for laziness), would get a result of 4,000. While an averagely intelligent child (barely a 5) for whom life does not do many favors (another scraped 5), but who is tremendously hardworking (let us give him or her a 10 for effort), gets a final result of 5,000.

Children need to be made to see that no amount of intelligence makes up for determination; that blistered fingers are a lot more worthy of respect than fingers covered in rings; that successful people always have one part of intuition but nine parts of obstinacy. And that includes poetry itself. Charles Baudelaire said as much to a woman who asked him what the muse was: "Inspiration, madame, is working every day."

Every day, every year, all through life. The other day I read somewhere that since the first oil well was discovered in 1857, 241 dry holes have been drilled for every well that has actually produced oil. Is life itself any more compliant than the earth? Are searchers after happiness any luckier than searchers after black gold? If those who drill for oil were as easily put off as those who study for a university degree, cars would still be running on dreams or on coal.

So tell the children: failing is only dangerous if, one, they laugh it off as a joke or, two, if they get comfortable with it. And tell them also that they are allowed to get disheartened when they have failed 242 times. Not before.

Traveling like suitcases

I imagine that the decrease in the value of the dollar will have slowed down the growing trend toward an increase in the number of tourists going abroad. I am not sure whether to be happy or sad, for foreign travel strikes me as being simultaneously one of the most laudable and one of the most difficult things a person can do. And my admiration for the traveler is matched only by my pity for the tourist.

The two things are not the same by any means, although they are often confused. The traveler moves through the world like a person reading a book, the tourist like someone simply watching television. Streets and people pass in front of the eyes of both, but while the traveler absorbs them into the pathways of the soul, the tourist simply flushes them down the drain of having a good time.

Johann von Goethe put it well, I think: "The person who journeys the world without having some great aim in mind would be better off staying at home." The real problem, then, is not where one travels, but why one travels, with what kind of spiritual predisposition one goes out into the world. Which is why the English say that travel is "good for the wise and bad for the stupid."

People who travel with an open mind—without rushing, knowing where they are going, reading about the cities they are going to visit before actually walking their streets— such people can have as many souls as countries that they visit. People like these will discover that travel expands ideas and shrinks prejudices, that it increases understanding and reduces selfishness. Travelers who prefer people to streets, streets to theaters, and theaters to idiotic spectacles have a good chance of coming back better people than when they left. People who travel to admire (not to spend time saying things like, "There's no place like home," or "For food, women, and sun, give me Florida every time"), people like these may perhaps get beyond the front page of the world that is their own country, which, no matter how beautiful it is, is still only the front page.

It is certainly not enough to travel. You have to know how to travel. And that is not something that you learn at school. To think that travel automatically broadens the mind is to forget Santiago Rusiñol's amusing phrase: "If it were true that travel broadens the mind, ticket collectors would be the wisest people in the world."

For there are people, and the majority of tourists do this, who travel as if they were simply having tickets clipped, as if they were suitcases. Suitcases crucified with labels and almost certainly containing only dirty clothes. Dirty clothes are all that a lot of people bring home after traveling all around Europe.

I am going to reproduce a paragraph by someone who hated tourists. It is a long paragraph, but I would ask the reader to read it carefully, for even though it rather exaggerates, it is priceless:

> What is it that makes most people travel? What could be more distressing, more annoying, more utterly banal, than the tourist? The tourist travels for reasons of vanity or fashion; he is the enemy of all who travel impelled by passion, by happiness or sadness, who travel to remember or to forget. The tourist is that ghastly unbearable individual who stares at the cobblestones in the street, who takes note of the greater or lesser comfort of the hotel where he is staying, and of the food. For there are actually people, and it is a ghastly thing to have to say,

who travel to try out different types of food. Others do it to frequent theaters, cafés, casinos, cabaret shows that are the same everywhere, and equally horrid and repulsive wherever they are to be found. And there are those who travel out of topophobia, running away from places, not traveling to get somewhere new but to escape from the place they have left. Many of those who travel are very often running from places: they cannot stay anywhere. It is not that they are drawn by the place they are heading for; they are simply repelled by the one they are leaving.

I would now ask the reader to reread the last lines of the paragraph carefully, for in them the philosopher puts his finger on one of the curses of our time: topophobia, or domophobia. How many people travel to escape from themselves, because they have ants in their pants, because they think that if they change climates they will change souls, because they cannot stand themselves or what is around them? Are they traveling? No, they are running. And what can you find when you are running?

Domophobia is a word that does not appear in the dictionary yet, but which has become fashionable recently thanks to certain psychiatrists and is one of the great illnesses of contemporary society. And a most remarkable phenomenon it is too, for the average standard of housing in the West has improved more in the last fifty years than in the twenty centuries that went before. The palaces of the rich may have lost something of their colossal size, but they have become much more habitable. And even the flats of the poor, bar a few exceptions, are a thousand miles away from the huts of a century ago, whose old Paleolithic kitchens now look like something out of a fairy tale. One would imagine that the jungle of gadgetry (televisions, radios, heaters, refrigerators, and the rest) might at long last have made homes out of mere dwellings.

But it transpires that it is precisely now that neither men nor women can bear to spend more than a few hours at home. The fashion is for the weekend flight to the swimming pool or the Sunday outing. Modern man, like a dog, has to be taken out for a walk every day.

So this is why traveling has become an escape. Not an opportunity for enriching the mind, but a mere flight from what we call "daily routine." For every ten decisions that people nowadays make, nine are motivated by the need to simply change position. It is not about choosing what we are getting; it is about leaving behind what we have. People nowadays cannot stand to be by themselves. Is it the world that is sick, or is it people's souls? Is it our eyes that do not see clearly, or is it that the reality surrounding us is jumbled and confused?

The poet Juan Ramón Jiménez, winner of the Nobel Prize, once told a young man that "in loneliness you find whatever you bring to it." Every traveler should be told the same: in the world you find what you carry in your heart: openness if your spirit is open, triviality and nonsense if it is without focus. That is why travelers who cannot stand being with themselves end up hating everything about their journey as well, and finish up talking the same nonsense as Alfonse Karr when he said, "In every country that we go to, one thing is superfluous: its inhabitants." For if I have no interest in the people who live in a country, how can I understand the houses they live in or the churches where they pray?

My friend, if you are not ready to travel, do not travel. First of all heal your soul, clean and exercise your eyes, and remember that your vices, your intransigent attitudes, and your lack of understanding will all be traveling with you. Do not traipse around the world with your bitterness; if you do, you will only spread it around and return with it grown even greater, for every country you visit will be a mirror that reflects your own inner poverty.

Only if you are happy, open, excited—if you want to learn and to love in other languages—only then set out; a wonderful world awaits you. And remember that only when you love your own home will the whole world become your home.

Our daily peace

My friend Joe Wrath is a fanatical antimilitarist. For years he has been obsessed by the topic of war. He knows by heart the number of nuclear warheads that each of the possible combatants has, where their missiles are located, the capacity of their aircraft carriers and their bombers, the total number of megatons that they could detonate.

But Joe is not satisfied with knowing the background; he acts on what he knows. No antiwar or ecological demonstration takes place without Joe's being there. He is an expert in placards, in slogans, in peace songs. He did not skip his compulsory military training because he did not discover the antiwar movement until years after doing it, although there are still times when he dreams of all the years he would have been able to spend in prison if he had known enough to play the noble role of the glorious objector.

To make up for lost time, Joe Wrath has chained himself to the gates of various barracks a total of four times now, taken part in several marches against nuclear energy plants, and participated in no fewer than forty-two anti-NATO demonstrations (he has counted them). He is proud to show off the scar (his "medal," he calls it) left by a rubber bullet on his right cheek and ear.

The funny thing is that Joe forgets all about his pacifism in his daily life, which, rather than being guided by his antiwar positions, seems rather to be under the "wrathful" influence of his last name. For Joe is argumentative and a troublemaker in his office, intolerant with his wife, harsh with his children, dismissive of his mother-in-law, and short with the doorman of the building where he lives and with his neighbors. All the peace that he dreams of for the world, he completely forgets about cultivating in his own home.

I am not writing this little parable in order to belittle public action against war (in a world as mad as the one in which we live, any service to peace deserves to be applauded), but rather to make the point that in the last instance the great peace of the world will only come about as the sum of the many millions of little fractions of peace that we bring into being in the lives of each of us. Many of our contemporaries live in fear that one day some fool of a soldier or politician will push a little button and blow the world to smithereens. But they do not realize that there are not one but three billion fools in the world, and that every day we push the button of our selfishness, which is a thousand times more dangerous than all the nuclear bombs put together. Of course I am concerned at the prospect of nuclear war. But I am a good deal more concerned by the fact that while we are all worrying about the great nuclear war, we do not even notice the thousands of little wars of nerves and tension in which we are permanently engaged.

How few peaceful and peace-giving souls one meets in everyday life! You talk to people and no sooner have you got going than they start on about their little hatreds and their fears. They show you their souls, and you see that if they are not studded with swords they are at the very least prickly with pins. What a delight it is, on the other hand, when you come across the kind of people who radiate serenity, people who are of course familiar with the evils of the world but who are not obsessed by them and who positively buzz with the will to live and to build! Some years ago a novel called *Peace Never Begins* was published. I would like to write one called *Peace Begins*

Within. For it seems to me that to believe nowadays that a possible future war depends above all on the nerves and toughness of Mr. Bush and Mr. Kameini is a simple excuse, in the same way that it is an excuse to put all the blame for past wars on Adolph Hitler or Joseph Stalin. All we are doing is creating scapegoats to free ourselves from our own responsibility. The world has violent leaders when the world itself is violent. If the world were peaceful, violent leaders would be biting their nails at home. War is not in the guns but in the souls of those who dream of firing them. And they do fire them.

That is why I like to see that when the dictionary defines the word *peace*, it also refers to inner peace, describing peace as "the state of being calm and quiet."

By this definition, the world is undoubtedly already at war. For nowadays, who enjoys the gift of a calm and rested spirit? Who does not live in a state of agitation, in the grip of passion? There was never so much distress or so much controversy; the kingdoms of anger and rage were never so extensive. And if you want proof, all you have to do is open a newspaper.

As you would expect, I am not talking about the false peace of the cemeteries, of that peace that the Latin poet Horace spoke of centuries ago: "They turn a land into a desert and call it peace." I am actually talking about peace as a flowering of life, in the same way as Baltasar Gracián, who said, "A man of great peace is a man of great vitality." Or if you prefer, about the best definition of peace that I know, the one given by St. Thomas Aquinas, who called it "the active calm of order in freedom." Nowadays it is no secret that we swing from order without freedom to freedom without order, and end up having neither calm nor action as a result.

We need to begin, it strikes me, by healing people's souls. By realizing that nobody but ourselves can bring us peace. The saying that you have to be ready to make war if you want to win peace is only true when it refers to the inner war against our own internal disarray.

The only genuine weapons against war are smiles and forgiveness, which together bring about tenderness. For that reason, someone who loves his or her spouse and children is much more antiwar than people who go on demonstrations. For the same reason, a good workmate who always has a ready joke does more good in the world than people who go around writing placards. The individual who listens to an old person and provides company to someone who is lonely is a thousand times more effective as a pacifist than a protester against the arms race. The commonest weapon in this century is the vinegar in people's souls, for it kills every day without ever declaring war.

I cannot help but be moved when I remember one of the great peacemakers of the twentieth century, our dear Pope John XXIII. He achieved a great deal, undoubtedly, with his *Pacem in terris*, but what else was this encyclical but the ideological working out and formalization of everything he had previously taught us with his smile? With a thousand people as serene, smiling, open, trusting, and humanly Christian as he was, the world would be saved. For it will not be saved by placards and demonstrations.

In praise of courage

When the winner of the Nadal Prize was announced, I imagine that a lot of people were struck by the fact that a woman, the mother of five children, had won two important literary prizes in the space of a month. But what most impressed me—being, as I am, a little strange—was the fact that the same woman, Carmen Gómez Ojea, had gone in for thirteen other competitions the previous year. Rather than being discouraged by her numerous failures, she went on fighting, hoping, and sending her work off to competitions. You certainly need to have quite exceptional courage to keep on believing in yourself and in your work after failing thirteen times. And you also need to maintain your faith in the honesty of other people, in order not to take the easy way out and resort to making comments like, "It's all a fix," or "You only get anywhere if you've got contacts."

The longer I live, the more I admire the passive virtues in a human being. When I was young, I used to value above all else genius, creativity, zeal, intelligence accompanied by enthusiasm. Now I give far more importance to patience, perseverance, the ability to take knocks, the gift of being able to stay optimistic and happy in the midst of difficulties.

Perhaps this is because life has taught me that it is quite possible to get lucky and have a first spectacular success, but that nothing truly solid and significant is ever created without swimming against the tide, without great doses of obstinacy and stubbornness. None of the geniuses whom I admire had it easy producing their work. Most of them had a very stormy time of it, and often they had to spend more time getting around problems than they did actually creating. It is even quite probable that they would never have produced any work at all if it had not been for all the setbacks they had to face.

Anton Bruckner's fifth symphony was on TV today, and the experience of listening to it was doubly enjoyable, first, because it is such a wonderfully beautiful work, but second, because I knew that the composer did not hear it performed in public until nineteen years after it had been written. And, like any writer or artist, I am also well familiar with the feeling of how a piece of work seems to rot away if you do not manage to have it performed or published. Not only does the passage of time not heal the wound; it actually seems as if what you have written swells up inside you, like a baby who is not born when his or her mother comes to term. You feel it dying inside you, you live as if burdened down with a corpse. And paradoxically, perhaps out of pity due to the fact that it has not managed to see the light, you become more and more convinced that that piece of work is the best thing you have ever done, in much the same way that all genuine parents feel a deep love for a child who is born handicapped. Your distress only gets worse as the years go by. You joke about it to yourself, you tell yourself that it will have finished its education by the time it is born, but you know perfectly well that these jokes are no more than an attempt to comfort yourself over the fate of this unborn child.

And it is all the worse if, as happened to Bruckner and so many other musicians, his work is relegated in this way because of the boorishness of a handful of critics whose names have only come down to us today because of the way they attacked these geniuses! Only an enormous faith in his work and in his duty to keep on creating could have kept Bruckner composing new symphonies while that miraculous fifth was hidden away.

And what about the ones who died without ever seeing the birth of their children? Gerald Manley Hopkins, a very influential nineteenth-century English poet (and whose influence went far beyond the English language), died without ever having had a single line published. He even suffered the bitter experience of having the most impressive and beautiful of all his poems, *The Wreck of the Deutschland*, rejected by a magazine run by his Jesuit colleagues, who completely failed to appreciate it.

Pierre Teilhard de Chardin also comes to mind. He had the boundless courage to write twenty or thirty volumes without getting a single one published in his lifetime. Could he have ever imagined that nowadays they would run to multiple editions in fifteen languages?

And now I think of Wolfgang Amadeus Mozart. There are days (not many, fortunately) when I get home absolutely destroyed by tiredness and by my failure to make myself understood. There are days when I wonder if it is worth struggling and writing, just so that such and such a bunch of fools can read you through muddy binoculars held back to front. On days like these, I have the most wonderful medicine at home: I sit down beside my record player and play the sonatas that Mozart wrote in the bitterest days of his life. The K. 545, for example, was composed just two days after one of his daughters died "of starvation," while his wife was at a spa, making a fool of him, flirting with anybody who was better off than he was. While she was doing that, Mozart would go hungry to rich people's houses and stuff his pockets with croquettes and sandwiches so as to have something to eat for the next few days. And I think all this while the most wonderful river of purity and joy pours from the loudspeakers (although there at bottom, in the adagios, you can hear Mozart's timid cry of pain and protest at this ill-constructed world that does not love him). How can anyone feel unfortunate at a time like that? How can I let my own tiny little ration of grief distract me for a single second from this wonderful calling of mine, which is to write and write?

There is no doubt about it: life is one long exercise in patience, and giving in to disheartenment is nothing but cowardice. How can we let the fact that we are not always properly understood stop us? Do we have so little faith in our own soul that we are rendered powerless by some act of injustice? Because one thing is clear: people who say they have lost their faith never had any real faith to lose. And those who lose faith in their calling never gave their faith the importance it deserves. To work for success, to work to win prizes—that is to rot. It is good to win from time to time, of course it is, for our human hearts are made of flesh, not steel. But we should live like flames. Flames never ask themselves whether their burning is important or not.

"Look after your wings, lad"

When St. Augustine gave young people the piece of advice that I have used as the title of this chapter, he was summing up, with all the usual efficiency of his literary style, a lifetime of human experience. I too would repeat it to all the young people who write to me: Look after your wings, or in the exact words of St. Augustine, "nourish and feed" your wings.

Perhaps one of the most striking aspects of the world in which we live is the large number of people who reach old age without ever realizing how hard their wings struggled to emerge from beneath their shoulder blades, only to die like dead branches, either because reality mutilated them or because their owners never took the trouble to look after them.

We should regard it as our duty to explain this matter to young people. For between the ages of fourteen and sixteen (I like to call this "the sacred age"), all normal human beings have the terrible gift of being able to choose between turning themselves into reptiles, who only use their legs to trip other people up, or into birds. The birds may fly more or less well, but all of them at the very least can get into the sky by their own efforts.

We should also explain even more clearly that when it comes down to it, the choice they make is almost completely up to them. We need to tell them that the world might trip them up, put obstacles in their way, make life difficult for them, render a good part of their efforts useless. But in the end it is they themselves who have the choice between making the leap or not, between accepting their wings or leaving them hanging on the clothes rack of mediocrity. It is the adolescent who chooses whether to creep or to fly.

I think we have gone from one extreme to the other in this matter. And I do not know which of the extremes is more dangerous. When I was passing through "the sacred age," some forty years ago now, we heard a lot of talk about "ideals." This was a wonderful gift, one for which I will never be able to express my thanks adequately. We were told that there were great principles for which it was worth fighting. Different kinds of heroism were pointed out to us, somewhat romantically, as goals that were possible and necessary in our own lives. Of course, there was a great deal of cliché and fantasy in it all. We had too many bright stars painted for us. But at least we got into the habit of looking upward.

What was never explained to us, on the other hand, and this was a mistake, was that reality is cruel and that three out of every four of our ideals would be mutilated or completely swept away. The number of times that we came up nil! And how many of us fell into the other extreme of cynicism!

But my impression is that nowadays exactly the opposite is happening, and this strikes me as being much more dangerous. Where are the masters or guides in the adult generation who have dreams worthy of being passed on? Is it not rather the case that young people are faced with a generation of weepers and wailers, people who cannot encourage them to fight, for the very simple reason that they no longer believe in the struggle themselves?

Earth has been overrun by what John XXIII called "the prophets of doom." Of course we all know that the planet is not exactly in a good way of going. But even so, you get up in the morning and the newspaper is predicting the next world war. The person sitting beside you on the bus tells you about how gas prices are going to go up. The woman who cleans the stairs complains that young people nowadays have no sense of respect, tidiness, or a dozen other things. A workmate moans about the boss, and you go into a bar and hear people bad-mouthing priests, politicians, the beer company, and chimney sweeps. By the time you get home in the evening, you wonder if anything at all works properly in the world; and you are amazed when you turn on the tap and it is water, not vinegar, that comes out.

Sometimes I feel sorry for young people today, for we have convinced them that the only future they have is the next world war and that while they wait for the bomb to fall they might as well waste their lives making as much noise as they possibly can.

I prefer to fly. And if the war that we are all afraid of does come, I hope that I will be flying at the time and that I will have lived to the full every moment of the life that was granted me. And if the war does not come, well, a world in which more and more people live their dreams is always going to be a lot better than one full of frightened reptiles.

That is why I tell young people to take care of their wings. And that they should try to have several pairs—three if possible, like seraphs—because real life always comes along and clips a couple, so you need to have some spare, just in case. And I also tell them never to forget that it is much more important to work at making wings than it is to try to get rid of your defects. There are people who spend their time taking stones out of their shoes or paring down their corns when all they need to do is simply to fly. It was St. Augustine who said, "Love, and do whatever you want," not because it is good to do whatever we want, but because if we love, we will only want to do worthwhile things, inspired by our faith.

If young people learned to fly, if they all nourished their wings, their courage, their passion, their desire to be somebody and to make the world a better place, it would not matter how many of them ended up unemployed, or how many drugs came pouring in along all the usual routes used by the traffickers. They would still believe in themselves and in their struggle. For it is not true that young people have problems because they start taking drugs or because they feel lonely. On the contrary: they get caught up in bitterness and drugs because they already have problems, because their souls are already half in chains. A jug has to be empty before you can fill it with poison or with vinegar. It takes a superb hunter to hit the birds that fly the highest. A lot of people complain about being walked on, without realizing that it was they themselves who chose to be cockroaches.

The heretic and the inquisitor

I think that somewhere I have told the old fable of the heretic and the inquisitor, a fable that made such an impression on me the first time I heard it. The story goes that many, many years ago a famous inquisitor died suddenly, just after getting home from an auto-da-fé at which a heretic whom he had condemned had been burned. The two of them arrived to be judged before God at exactly the same time; and, like all men, they stood naked before the tribunal. God began the trial asking what they thought of him, and the heretic started into a complicated speech explaining his theories about God, the very theories that had got him condemned on earth. God listened to him in amazement, for no matter how many questions he asked or how many detailed answers the heretic gave, God did not understand what the heretic meant, nor did he recognize anything of himself in the heretic's explanations. The inquisitor spoke next, all full of pride. He laid out the whole elaborate orthodox position before God, the same position that he had demanded that the heretic accept and for which he had ordered him to be burned when he had refused. And he was amazed to discover that God did not understand what he was talking about either, and that God still did not recognize anything of himself in the picture that the strictly orthodox inquisitor was painting. "Which of the two of you is the heretic?" God wondered, without being able to make up his mind. For both of them struck God as being either heretics, madmen, or just plain frauds, he was not sure which.

It was getting late, and the more explanations that the two of them gave, the clearer it became that neither of them knew much about God, not to mention the fact that it became impossible to tell who was the heretic and who the inquisitor. So God resorted to the ultimate test and asked the angels to remove both of their hearts and bring them to him. And that was when it was discovered that neither of them had a heart at all.

I say that this fable, of whose orthodoxy I am not entirely convinced myself, made such an impression on me when I first heard it because I am sure that on the day of judgment God is going to pay a lot more attention to our hearts than to our ideas, while here on earth we spend half our lives fighting over our ideas and not bothering to love each other in the meantime.

It is said that on one occasion Papal Nuncio Angelo Roncalli (who was later to become John XXIII) was seated at a banquet next to a famous politician whose ideas were not exactly close to those of a bishop. After talking about all matters high and low for several hours, somebody heard the nuncio smilingly say to his companion, "When it comes down to it, the only difference between you and me is our ideas."

It is not that Roncalli did not consider ideas to be important; he just did not give them the position of unique importance that we normally accord them in the world. He was well aware that even for two people of quite radically different ideas, there can be a thousand routes to reconciliation. He knew that when two people love each other, they start to draw closer to each other even in their ideas, or else they discover that their ideas were not so different as they had imagined. On the other hand, a pair of cold hearts will end up falling out, even when they think the same.

It is true; we have given too much importance to thought and intelligence, which are neither the only qualities of a human being nor the most important ones. There is a lot more to a human being than the contents of his or her head, fortunately. Above all, a lot more than mere dogmatically held opinions.

And yet not only do we often require other people to share our opinions; we also demand that they have the same way of thinking and expressing themselves as we do. That is the reason why ninety-nine out of every hundred fights that happen between people are caused by mere words, by matters of no substance, by ways of expressing ourselves.

The problem with dogmatic opinions is not that the people who hold them passionately defend certain ideas (I would even regard this as positive). The problem is that they begin by defending ideas but then go on to defend their own particular way of understanding and expressing these ideas. Then they start to get the ideas mixed up with their own personal obsessions. Then they finally end up forcing everybody else to accept the ideas, their way of expressing them, and their own personal obsessions, all jumbled up together.

When, on the other hand, people try to love their enemies, they begin by realizing they do not have enemies, but adversaries. They then go on to find that the other side is also partly right. The next stage is to understand that at bottom their competitor's ideas and their own are not so different, and they end up discovering that they can work together with their adversary in an area that lies beyond any differences they might have.

Somebody once explained to me that the best way to collect water in your hands without its escaping is to join your hands in such a way that the fingers of your right hand fit into the spaces between the fingers of your left hand and vice versa so that they form a kind of bowl, or cradle. It is impossible to close your hands completely if you place your fingers tip to tip, index finger to index finger, middle finger to middle finger, ring finger to ring finger. Just imagine how well marriages could work if only husband and wife complemented each other like two hands, covering up each other's gaps and errors!

In the church we are only now coming to understand (five centuries late!) that Martin Luther's doctrines were not so far from the Catholic position as was thought five hundred years ago, or as we ourselves had thought. What happens is that controversy increases differences to the same degree that love diminishes and lessens them.

Raoul Follereau has a book entitled *Loving One Another Is the Only Truth,* an assertion that strikes me as being absolutely correct. The inquisitors appear to the right and left of love. And a lot of those who think that they are fighting dogmatism end up being just as dogmatic themselves, albeit in defense of ideas of a different hue.

I adore people who love, even if I do not share their ideas. For I know that love is the only letter that always arrives, even if it has the wrong address written on it. Truth without love, on the other hand, no matter how truthful it may be, will quickly become a sword, a "Take that, whether you like it or not," a dose of castor oil, a caricature of the truth.

My ten commandments

Some radio station or other has called me to ask what my ten commandments are. Apparently they are contacting various people to ask what commandments they would make compulsory so that the world could be a better place. I find the idea amusing, for it appeals to the little dictator that all of us have hidden away inside. Who among us would not love to be God for half an hour, in the conviction that we could make a much better job of organizing the world than the real God does? Who has not in his or her heart drawn up laws and plans to "redirect" human freedom, put an end to violence, or banish loneliness? The world is full of little gods, and all of us have within us to some extent a little altar upon which we worship ourselves.

Personally I do not feel qualified to draw up a set of ten commandments. God only knows what silly ideas my quirky mind would come up with and then start forcing on other people! And God also knows that when we humans gain power over others (just think of all the dictators and petty tyrants of history), our legacy is usually horror, even though we occasionally manage to camouflage it beneath a veneer of public order, like the icing on a cake!

That is why I told the people from the radio station that I think that the ten commandments in the Bible are "pretty adequate" and that I really do not have the energy to try to "improve" them. I have enough to do just trying to keep the commandments that God gave without starting to force ten of my own on other people.

But I did not want to disappoint the people from the radio station either, so I told them that what I do have is my own personal interpretation of the original commandments; an interpretation that I logically regard as binding only for myself, since I have always thought that getting my own house in order is the best place to start.

So just in case it might be of some use to someone else, here is my interpretation. I offer it in the hope that it might help other people to come up with their own.

1. Love God, José Luis. Love God without great high-sounding words, as you love your father or a friend. Never hold to a faith that does not show itself through love. Always remember that your God is not something unreal, an abstraction, the logical conclusion of some clever syllogism, but rather someone who loves you and whom you should love. Do not forget that a God who cannot be loved does not deserve to exist. Love God as you know how to: humbly. And be happy giving all the love that is in your heart to God, your fellow human beings, Mozart, and your cat in equal measure. And at the same time as you love God, stay away from all the idols that the world sets up, those idols that will never give you love but that could come to control you completely: power, comfort, money, cheap emotion, violence.

2. Do not use important words lightly: *God, country, love.* Touch on these grand matters in the same way that the main bell in the cathedral gets rung: only on special occasions and with great respect. Never use them against other people, never for mere effect, and never to your own advantage. Remember that using them as a shield to

defend yourself or as a javelin to hurl at others is one of the cruelest forms of blasphemy.

3. Always remember that Sunday is a fine invention and that you are not a beast of burden that exists only to sweat and die. Force yourself to set aside that heavy workload that hounds and harasses you, and make time for silence, for music, for nature, for your own soul, for God, when all is said and done. You know that there are flowers in your soul that only grow when you work. Just do not forget that there are others that only live in the fertile ground of leisure.

4. Bear in mind that you inherited what is best in you from your mother and your father. And since you no longer have the good fortune to be able to show your love for them in this world, allow the memory of them to continue to mold your life. You know very well, José Luis, that you will never be able, by your own efforts alone, to reach the levels of love and tenderness that your mother gave you or the honesty and love for work that your father taught you.

5. Do not forget that you were born a carnivore, that you are by nature aggressive, and that for this reason it is easier for you to kill than to love. Stay alert and make sure you do no harm to any person, animal, or thing. You know that sometimes you can kill just by smiling and saying no, and that the only way to be sure that you have not killed anyone is to give your whole life over to helping others.

6. Never accept the idea that life is like a cowboy film, where the soul is the good guy and the body the bad. Your body is as pure as your soul and needs to be looked after just as carefully. So do not be afraid of friendship or love: respect

them precisely because you value them. But never fall into the great trap of thinking that love is about getting pleasure for yourself, when really it is about giving happiness to others.

7. Do not deprive anyone of the right to be free. Do not allow anyone to deprive you of your right to freedom and happiness. Remember that you were granted a soul so that you could share it, and that anyone who does not share his or her soul is committing robbery, just like a river that goes stagnant and rotten when it does not run.

8. Remember that of all the weapons you have, your tongue is the most dangerous. Worship truth, but do not forget two things: you will never find perfect truth, and you should never try to force your version of truth on others.

9. Do not desire your neighbor's wife, his house, his car, his video equipment, or his salary. Never allow your heart to become a dumping ground for junk and stupid desires.

10. Do not be jealous of other people's property or of your own. Only allow yourself to be mean with one thing: your time. Fill the years you have been granted with life. Remember that only those who wish for nothing possess everything. And always remember that no matter what happens, you will always have what is most important: the love of your Father, who is in heaven, and the company of other people, who are on earth.

José Luis Martín Descalzo — A Life Sketch

José Luis Martín Descalzo was born in Madridejos, a little village in the middle of Spain, on August 27, 1930. While he was still a baby, his family moved north and settled in Astorga, a rural town. There he would enjoy a happy childhood against the bloody background of the Spanish Civil War. Soon he joined the seminary to become a priest. After studying in Astorga and Valladolid, he was sent to Rome to finish his studies. While in Rome, where he obtained an S.T.L. and S.T.D. in church history, he was ordained a priest in 1953.

Upon his return to Spain, he worked at *El Norte de Castilla*, the main newspaper in Valladolid. During this time he worked on a novel, *La frontera de Dios*. His friends told him not to present it to receive a prestigious literary award. Not paying attention to them, he went ahead and received the first-place prize. His activity as a journalist continued in a Bilbao newspaper. While working there, he was sent to Rome as the reporter to cover the Second Vatican Council, where he did an outstanding job. In 1966 he received a degree in journalism and began working for *ABC*, Spain's leading newspaper at the time. As its religious reporter, he had the opportunity to accompany Pope Paul VI in all his travels.

In 1968 José Luis became the director of the weekly magazine *Vida Nueva*, a position he held until 1975. These were transition years both for the Catholic church and for Spain. The church lived through a period of upheaval following the changes envisioned by the Second Vatican Council. Spain lived the final years of the dictatorship of Francisco Franco and the beginnings of a new yet fragile democracy. José Luis Martín Descalzo tried to be true to his times and to his church. As he would often say, "God does not belong either to the right or to the left," and "Renovation does not mean destruction, but let no one tell us, for the sake of faithfulness, to become a mere rerun of the past." He was deeply committed to the renewal of the Spanish church in light of his experience at Vatican II. This commitment was the source of frequent criticism on the part of those who considered themselves to be guardians of the church.

Already in the 1970s he was a well-known journalist and his articles were published not only in Spain, but also in Argentina, Chile, Venezuela, and Colombia. During the 1980s he continued his work at *ABC*, where his weekly column reached millions of readers and was the origin of his *Reasons*. At the same time, he began broadcast of *Pueblo de Dios*, a television program on religion and society.

His final years were conditioned by a series of kidney problems and a heart disease. His experience of illnesses and suffering led him to write more and to write better. He lived his suffering and his cross with love and passion, transforming them into poetry. His *Testamento de un pájaro solitario* is the final witness of this human being, a hymn to life as he faced death. He passed away on June 26, 1991.

His literary production comprises all kinds of work. He wrote poetry (*Fábulas con Dios al fondo* [*Fables with God on the Background*], *Querido mundo terrible* [*Dear Terrible World*], *Testamento de un pájaro solitario* [*The Will of a Lonely Bird*]); drama (*La hoguera feliz* [*The Happy Fire*], *Segundo juicio de Galileo* [*Galileo's Second Trial*], *Las prostitutas os precederán en el Reino de los cielos* [*Prostitutes Will Precede You in the Kingdom of Heaven*]); and novels (*La frontera de Dios* [*God's Frontier*], *El hombre que no sabía pecar* [*The Man Who Did Not Know How to Sin*], *El demonio de media tarde* [*The Devil in Mid-Afternoon*]). He also wrote literary essays such as *Un cura se confiesa* (*A Priest Makes His Confession*), *Un periodista en el Concilio* (*A Journalist at the Council*), and *Vida y misterio de Jesús de Nazareth* (*Life and Mystery of Jesus of Nazareth*). He was also author of several movie scripts.

Index

Acceptance, 69, 70, 73, 90, 122
Adam, K., 115
Alférez, A., 117
Andreiev, L., 111
Appearances, 37, 45
Azorín (J. M. Ruiz), 134

Bacon, F., 47, 84
Balmes, J., 134
Balzac, H. de, 51
Baudelaire, Ch., 136
Becket, S., 51
Beethoven, L., 26, 135
Bernanos, G., 6, 31, 39, 60, 70, 88,
    112, 125
Bible, 84, 157
Body, 10, 72, 121–24, 159
Bruckner, A., 146

Caiaphas, 111
Calderón de la Barca, P., 26
Camus, A., 31
Carnegie, D., 78
Casona, A., 75
Cervantes, M., 26
Christmas, 27, 57–60, 61–63
Cirolli, D., 65
Courage, 24, 39, 43, 81, 100, 145,
    147, 151

Darío, R., 78
Death, 13, 15, 20, 30, 34–35, 51,
    52, 75, 84, 86, 113–16, 118,
    119, 123, 124, 126
Dolto, F., 81
Dreams, 12, 21, 30, 43, 70, 100
Duquoc, C., 115

Easter, 109, 114, 117
Easter Sunday, 117
Effort, 44, 91, 130
Einstein, A., 134

Failure, 22, 70, 106, 133–34
Faith, 9, 18, 39, 47, 60, 66, 71, 79,
    107, 120, 123, 131, 145–48,
    158
Fear, 8, 13–15, 51, 52, 60, 78, 98,
    102, 142
Ferrari, E., 123
Follereau, R., 156
Forgiveness, 35, 90–92, 103, 144
Forman, T., 121
Freedom, 26, 83, 92, 97–100, 114,
    115, 123, 130, 131, 143, 157,
    160
Freud, S., 83
Friendship, 14, 53–56, 106, 107,
    111, 159

Gala, A., 77
García Lorca, F., 134
Generosity, 12, 62, 78, 114
Gironella, J. M., 29, 32
God, 10, 15, 16, 18, 31, 34, 40, 46,
   57–60, 61–63, 70, 71, 78–80,
   92, 95, 103, 108, 115, 117,
   122–23, 126–27, 130–32, 152,
   154, 157–59
Goethe, J. W. von, 92, 99, 137
Gómez de la Serna, R., 134
Gómez Ojea, C., 145
Gonzalo de Berceo, 116
Good Friday, 109, 114, 115, 118
Goretti, E., 41
Grace, 42, 44, 130
Gracián, B., 143
Greene, G., 13, 15, 19, 92
Grotjahn, M., 78
Guardini, R., 111
Guillén, J., 126

Habit, 6, 50–51, 98
Happiness, 28, 39, 41, 58–60, 71,
   78, 107, 108, 118, 120, 123,
   127, 136, 138, 160
Hatred, 74, 103, 110
Hernando, B., 78
Honesty, 11, 145, 159
Honor, 37, 39, 40, 113
Hope, 14–16, 24, 39, 58, 60, 87,
   100, 107, 108, 120
Hopkins, G. M., 147
Horace, 143
Huarte de san Juan, J., 37

Ideals, 21, 23, 27, 150
Intolerance, 90, 130, 131

Jesus Christ, 19, 42, 62, 100, 101,
   103, 109, 110–11, 114–16,
   118–20
Jiménez, J. R., 141
Joan of Arc, 18
John Paul II, 92
John XXIII, 144, 150, 154
Joubert, J., 135
Joy, 27, 30, 33, 56, 91, 124, 147
Judas, 109–12
Judgment, 11, 153
Justice, 10, 12, 22, 23, 39, 43, 131

Kafka, F., 83
Karr, A., 140
Kazantzakis, N., 71
Kierkegaard, S., 17

Lanza del Vasto, G. G. L. E. Lanza
   di Trabia, 111
Laughter, 77–80
Lazarus, 119, 126
Lombardi, L., 83
Loneliness, 34, 76, 105–08, 140,
   144, 152, 157
Love, 13–15, 18, 20, 23, 32, 34, 35,
   39, 43, 59–60, 66, 67, 70–71,
   82–84, 98–100, 108, 110, 111,
   112, 114, 116, 117, 126–27,
   146, 147, 151, 155, 156, 157–
   60

Machado, A., 16, 28
Machiavelli, N., 46

Marini, F., 45

Marshall, B., 79

Marsillach, A., 47

Marx Brothers, 45

Mozart, W. A., 134, 147, 158

Nietzsche, F., 58

Ochoa, S., 68

Parenthood, 27, 42–43, 70, 81–84, 89, 90, 99, 133–34, 146

Patience, 145, 148

Peace, 23, 24, 31, 42, 102, 141–44

Péguy, Ch., 81

Peñalosa, J. A., 121

Perseverance, 145

Pirandello, L., 51

Plato, 19

Queiroz, E., 78

Quevedo, F., 26

Resurrection, 109, 118–20

Ricciotti, G., 111

Rosales, L., 31, 58

Routine, 50, 52, 98, 140

Rusiñol, S., 138

St. Augustine, 91, 149, 151

St. Francis of Assisi, 79

St. Maria Goretti, 42

St. Paul the Apostle, 113

St. Teresa of Avila, 26, 125, 127, 130

St. Thomas Aquinas, 143

Salvation, 21, 114, 119, 130

Schiller, F., 82

Schweitzer, A., 21

Selfishness, 10, 12, 14, 28, 29, 32, 63, 75, 83, 102, 106, 142

Seneca, 99

Shaw, G. B., 135

Silence, 17, 110, 159

Smile, 15, 19, 77–79, 87, 102, 144

Suffering, 4, 14, 35, 52, 55, 56, 75, 86, 88, 89, 118, 125, 133

Teilhard de Chardin, P., 147

Terrorism, 34, 35, 58, 73–76

Trust, 6, 7, 8, 22, 23, 122

Truth, 19, 22, 39, 62, 92, 131, 156, 160

Vallejo, C., 86

Violence, 6, 33, 34, 35, 50, 101, 102, 103, 114, 157, 158

War, 1, 29–31, 60, 74, 75, 93, 96, 97, 130, 141–44, 151

Wilde, O., 107

Work, 23, 26, 39, 41, 42, 43, 90, 94, 95, 97, 98, 100, 134, 135, 148, 159

Yourcenar, M., 97

Yupanqui, A., 61